THE EVERYTHING

EASY WORD SEARCH BOOK
VOLUME II

Dear Reader,

Let's have some fun! I've designed these word search puzzles to be nice and mellow. You'll still be challenged, but in an enjoyable way. Unlike some puzzle books, this one is meant to make you feel good. You can pleasantly lose yourself in a sea of letters as you find the words. Then return to the real world feeling refreshed and a little sharper.

Children instinctively know that playing helps their brains grow. They play for fun, not for practical reasons. Solving word search puzzles is similar—it's a fun activity that can give our brains a boost. Research indicates that this kind of mental aerobics is healthy for kids of all ages.

I've created dozens of word search books and it was a pleasure making this one for you. Each puzzle has a theme and I cover a wide variety of interesting topics. I hope you find the journey through these pages rewarding. Have fun!

Charles Timmerman

Welcome to the EVERYTHING® Series!

These handy, accessible books give you all you need to tackle a difficult project, gain a new hobby, comprehend a fascinating topic, prepare for an exam, or even brush up on something you learned back in school but have since forgotten.

You can choose to read an Everything® book from cover to cover or just pick out the information you want from our four useful boxes: e-questions, e-facts, e-alerts, and e-ssentials. We give you everything you need to know on the subject, but throw in a lot of fun stuff along the way, too.

We now have more than 400 Everything® books in print, spanning such wide-ranging categories as weddings, pregnancy, cooking, music instruction, foreign language, crafts, pets, New Age, and so much more. When you're done reading them all, you can finally say you know Everything®!

PUBLISHER Karen Cooper

MANAGING EDITOR, EVERYTHING® SERIES Lisa Laing

COPY CHIEF Casey Ebert

ASSOCIATE PRODUCTION DDITOR Mary Beth Dolan

ACQUISITIONS EDITOR Lisa Laing

EVERYTHING® SERIES COVER DESIGNER Erin Alexander

Visit the entire Everything® series at *www.everything.com*

THE
EVERYTHING®
EASY WORD SEARCH BOOK
VOLUME II

Over 200 easy word search puzzles

Charles Timmerman, Founder of Funster.com

Adams Media

New York   London   Toronto   Sydney   New Delhi

Dedicated to White Bear

Adams Media
An Imprint of Simon & Schuster, Inc.
57 Littlefield Street
Avon, Massachusetts 02322

For information about special discounts for bulk purchases, please contact Simon & Schuster Special Sales at 1-866-506-1949 or business@simonandschuster.com.

The Simon & Schuster Speakers Bureau can bring authors to your live event. For more information or to book an event contact the Simon & Schuster Speakers Bureau at 1-866-248-3049 or visit our website at www.simonspeakers.com.

Manufactured in the United States of America

10 9 8 7 6 5 4 3

Library of Congress Cataloging-in-Publication Data has been applied for.

ISBN 978-1-4405-5674-6

Contents

Acknowledgments

I would like to thank each and every one of the more than half a million people who have visited my website, *www.funster.com*, to play word games and puzzles. You have shown me how much fun puzzles can be and how addictive they can become!

It is a pleasure to acknowledge the folks at Adams Media who made this book possible. I particularly want to thank my editor, Lisa Laing, for so skillfully managing the many projects we have worked on together.

Introduction

THE PUZZLES IN THIS book are in the traditional word search format. Words in the list are hidden in the puzzle in any direction: up, down, forward, backward, or diagonally. The words are always found in a straight line and letters are never skipped. Words can overlap. For example, the two letters at the end of the word "MAST" could be used as the start of the word "STERN." Only uppercased letters are used, and any spaces in an entry are removed. For example, "TROPICAL FISH" would be found in the puzzle as "TROPICALFISH." Apostrophes and hyphens are also omitted in the puzzles. Draw a circle around each word that you find. Then cross the word off the list so that you will always know which words remain to be found.

A favorite strategy is to look for the first letter in a word, then see if the second letter is in any of the neighboring letters, and so on until the word is found. Or instead of searching for the first letter in a word, it is sometimes easier to look for letters that stand out, like Q, U, X, and Z. Double letters in a word will also stand out and be easier to find. Another strategy is to simply scan each row, column, and diagonal looking for any words.

PUZZLES

Jams and Jellies

```
R A S P B E R R Y T S A T F
B P I R A P B E S B S F O R
R P B E G A I D L J Y R C U
A L S S E R S A L A E O I I
B E P E L G C L O R N V R T
U L L R H K U A R S T A P N
H T U V B C I M E E U L A A
R E M E G H T R D J H F Y R
A M R S B A V A U G C K P R
O R A N G E M M B V C M E U
Y U O C S E R G N I N N A C
F O X M M S U R T I C I C B
V G T O A S T S Y R R E H C
P D H C I W D N A S U G A R
```

APPLE	CHUTNEYS	JARS	STICKY
APRICOT	CITRUS	MARMALADE	SUGAR
AROMA	CONSERVES	ORANGE	TASTY
BAGEL	CURRANT	PEACH	TOAST
BATCHES	FLAVOR	PLUM	
BISCUIT	FRUIT	PRESERVES	
BLACKBERRY	GOURMET	RASPBERRY	
BLUEBERRY	GRAPE	RHUBARB	
CANNING	GUAVA	ROLLS	
CHERRY	HOMEMADE	SANDWICH	

Solution on page 245

Writing Utensils

```
T H D Q U I L L E A D W K Z
H Y I R E S A R E T T O L B
E G N G L Q D V Y Z O D O A
S R V E H H S U R B K I Q M
A A I M P L E M E N T C S B
U P X G D D I T I A R T U O
R H P E E I O G B E A I T O
U I L L V N E L H T T O A C
S T E L I K E C I T N N R T
T E T R C A T O O L E A A T
Y N S H E E N J K U M R P S
L M A R K E R C S N G Y P M
I I P S R R U L E R I X A W
R N O Y A R C T D E P B X P
```

APPARATUS	DICTIONARY	MARKER	STATIONERY
APPLIANCE	DYE	NIB	STYLI
BAMBOO	ERASER	NOTEBOOK	TABLE
BLOTTER	GEL	PASTEL	THESAURUS
BRUSH	GRAPHITE	PEN	TOOL
CHAIR	HIGHLIGHTER	PIGMENT	WAX
CRAYON	IMPLEMENT	QUILL	
DESK	INK	RULER	
DEVICE	LEAD	SKETCHER	

Solution on page 245

Photography Class

```
A B S T R A C T M U I D E M
F I L M X P O H S O T O H P
R E G R A L N E B N M O O Z
O G N I G D O D E O S R T D
R E G S E G A M I I E H E G
C L O S E U P L L T G E L N
A U P B M O O H E I P W A I
M P L U L F O M L S M O N P
E U B E T U T K O O N D D P
R L V R E H C S D P J A S O
A E O T G A I E P M K H C R
D P T I B T R I P O D S A C
P E L G N I S S E C O R P A
S C I T P O T O H P E L E T
```

ABSTRACT	DODGING	OPTICS
ALBUM	ENLARGER	PHOTOSHOP
ANSEL ADAMS	FILM	PORTFOLIO
BACKLIGHT	IMAGES	PROCESSING
BLUR	ISO SPEED	SHADOW
CAMERA	LANDSCAPE	SILHOUETTE
CLOSE UP	LIGHT METER	SPOOL
COMPOSITION	MACRO	TELEPHOTO
CROPPING	MEDIUM	TRIPOD
DEVELOPMENT	MODE	ZOOM

Solution on page 245

Going to the Movies

```
C E E N I T A M H O R R O R
I P O P C O R N O I T C A E
T A I E R U T N E V D A S M
N T N Q H O L L Y W O O D A
A O D C R E D I T S D M F K
M L I N E E R U T A E F O E
O R E T S U B K C O L B R M
R F E D A T E L N T C E E I
C R S S U M A E E A I B I T
O I P Q T S I K U M C O G W
M E I U S R C N E Q L H N O
E N L I N I O R A X R E O H
D D C E T U P O Z V T A E S
Y S A T N A F A M I L Y M R
```

ACTION	FANTASY	MATINEE	SEAT
ADVENTURE	FEATURE	NACHOS	SHOWTIME
ANIMATION	FOREIGN	POPCORN	SODA
BLOCKBUSTER	FRIENDS	PREMIERE	TICKET
CLASSICS	FUN	PRODUCTION	
CLIPS	HOLLYWOOD	QUIET	
COMEDY	HORROR	REEL	
CREDITS	INDIE	REMAKE	
DATE	LINE	RESTROOM	
FAMILY	MARQUEE	ROMANTIC	

Solution on page 245

Pizzeria

```
V O A D O S A U C E N E V O
S E L B A T O M A T O H S Y
E D S O G A M E S R E P A C
T N O C A B E E F L I S A B
A M O O R H S U M N O I N O
L P A Z V A O N A G E R O X
P L A R L M P C A H G U O D
N I H T I A H D P P D Q N R
C D G S R N C H I C K E N I
C R U S T O A T Z N H I M N
C I L R A G N R Z F I E N K
P E P P E R L S A E A N W S
Y F D O L I V E A T I N G Y
J Z E Y T S A T S A P N U F
```

BACON	DRINKS	NAPKINS	SAUCE
BASIL	EATING	OLIVE	SODA
BEEF	FETA	ONION	SPINACH
BOX	FUN	OREGANO	TABLES
CALZONE	GAMES	OVEN	TASTY
CAPERS	GARLIC	PARSLEY	THIN
CHEWY	HAM	PASTA	TOMATO
CHICKEN	HOT	PATRONS	
CRUST	MARINARA	PEPPER	
DINING	MEATS	PIZZA	
DOUGH	MUSHROOM	PLATES	

Solution on page 246

Red Cross to the Rescue

```
G B L O O D C A N I R T A K
I R A V T R O P P U S H Y P
F M E R O C M O S T U T E L
H U A N T L M O L M E F Y E
Z T N N A O U I A F I E C H
D E L D U C N N A L K K N O
O I C A S S I S T A N C E S
N T S N E T T R U E R H G P
A O C A A H Y Q R Y E A R I
T R W R S L H D C U D R E T
I N I A O T U N E C H I M A
O A N U R S E B P E Q T E L
N D I A H G S R M I N Y N N
P O E D A N O I T A C U D E
```

AGENCY	DONATION	KATRINA
AID	EARTHQUAKE	LIFE
AMBULANCE	EDUCATION	NEEDY
ASSISTANCE	EMERGENCY	NURSE
BARTON	FLOOD	RED
BLOOD	FUNDS	SAFETY
CHARITY	HEALTH	SUPPORT
COMMUNITY	HELP	TORNADO
CPR	HOSPITAL	TSUNAMI
CROSS	HUMANITARIAN	VOLUNTEER
DISASTER	HURRICANE	WAR

Solution on page 246

Write a Letter

```
L I C N E P C O M P O S E I
R E C O N N E C T I O N P N
S H P A R G A R A P Q S O C
S E E M L C N N F K N I L R
E A N R A L O E R U T G E E
R R P L E T I N P A M N V A
D T A O E Q S G T I E E N T
D F L V D L U U R A S D E I
A E R E V I L E D A C T V V
I L S D R A C T S O P T L E
E T A K S M N S O T O H P E
T H A N K Y O U S T O R Y A
A P O S T S C R I P T Y P E
D N E S E L D O O D Y D O B
```

ADDRESS	ENVELOPE	POSTCARD
BODY	EPISTLE	POSTSCRIPT
CALLIGRAPHY	HEARTFELT	RECONNECTION
COMPOSE	INK	REQUEST
CONCLUSION	LOVE	SALUTATION
CONTACT	MAIL	SEND
CREATIVE	NOTE	SIGNED
DATE	PARAGRAPHS	STAMP
DEAR	PEN PAL	STORY
DELIVER	PENCIL	THANK YOU
DESK	PERFUME	TYPE
DOODLES	PHOTOS	

Solution on page 246

Convenience Store

```
I A L C O H O L O T T E R Y
C L B B H G U M I D O O F K
O I N E P O S Y A W L A R U
R G T V B A C O F F E E E B
N H M E G G R O C E R I E S
E T A R E M A C L I C E Z E
R E P A P S W E N A R N E I
E R S G A D O S U F T R R T
S S E E Y O L P M E B E D L
T W T S O U V E N I R S R E
R E I H S A C T A D E L I V
O E C H I P S R E T A W N O
O T Y F U E L C A N D Y K N
M S T N I M S N A C K L I M
```

ALCOHOL	DELI	MAPS
ALWAYS OPEN	DRINK	MILK
BEER	EMPLOYEES	MINTS
BEVERAGES	FOOD	NEWSPAPER
BREAD	FREEZER	NOVELTIES
CAMERA	FUEL	RESTROOM
CANDY	GAS	SLUSHY
CASHIER	GROCERIES	SNACK
CHIPS	GUM	SODA
CHOCOLATE	ICE	SOUVENIRS
COFFEE	LIGHTERS	SWEETS
CORNER	LOTTERY	WATER

Solution on page 246

Airport Runway

```
G N O L E L L A R A P F S S
H S E C U R I T Y N A L A G
D E P A R T U R E L T A F N
U N O I T C E R I D H T E I
Y A W I X A T L I F T R T K
L L J O G N I Y L F T O Y R
A P E T D G H C A O R P A A
N R T V H H L R W E G R V M
D I S T A N C E P K E I K P
I A I A Y R R U W A A A G I
N N F M I K G P O T R A A L
G T L A H P S A I T T U C O
T E T E R C N O C E M E N T
C A M R A T N E M E V A P S
```

AIRCRAFT	DISTANCE	LONG	TARMAC
AIRPLANES	FAA	MARKINGS	TAXIWAY
AIRPORT	FLAT	PARALLEL	TOUCHDOWN
APPROACH	FLYING	PATH	TOWER
ASPHALT	GATE	PAVEMENT	
AVIATION	GEAR	PILOTS	
CEMENT	GRAVEL	SAFETY	
CONCRETE	JETS	SECURITY	
DEPARTURE	LANDING	SKY	
DIRECTION	LIGHTING	TAKEOFF	

Solution on page 247

Knitting Needle

```
T D L V A R T L G L K Y H V
D O O W O M J Y W N N O T W
W R O L O Y D S D J I U G G
P O O L B L A N K E T W N T
A C R B M F Q E A N S K E P
I E O K A F G T F R T I L S
R H Z B B U V T S E G A G S
S C R T A H N I F T S W H N
O I A G H U N M S T I T C H
C S V B O G A W I A N H P O
K R T C L L I C Z P N I L O
S V A E F E A B E E N N O K
N E M F S X Q C T R A P N P
T S L A T E M W E A V E G W
```

ART	GAUGE	METAL	SINGLE
BAMBOO	GRANDMA	MITTENS	SIZE
BIGHT	HAT	PAIR	SOCKS
BLANKET	HOBBY	PATTERN	STITCH
CABLE	HOOK	PIN	TAPER
COLOR	KNIT	PLASTIC	THIN
COUNT	LACE	POINT	TOOL
CRAFT	LENGTH	ROD	WEAVE
DESIGN	LONG	SETS	WOOD
FABRIC	LOOP	SEWING	WORK

Solution on page 247

Educational

```
C K R O W E M O H C A O C N
L C O N T E N T L I C N E P
A S H O W X N I A L P X E A
S E T N B E B M U E S U M C
S R I M P R O V I N G U A A
K U P R A C T I C E P V D D
L T R R O I G E L L E L V E
E C I U K S E N I Z A G A M
S E L D A E S F I R V N N I
S L O E R S T E U Y R Q C C
O L O M D I E T F A F U E M
N I H A N O L H E O V I D A
S K C G V U M L T Y R Z D X
B S S T C U R T S N I P W E
```

ACADEMIC
ADVANCED
BOOK
CLASS
COACH
CONTENT
CULTURAL
DRILLS
EDIFYING
EXAM
EXERCISES

EXPLAIN
GAME
HOMEWORK
IMPROVING
INSTRUCT
LEARN
LECTURES
LESSONS
LIBRARIES
MAGAZINES
MODEL

MUSEUM
PENCIL
PRACTICE
PROFESSOR
QUIZ
SCHOOL
SHOW
SKILL
THESAURUS
UPLIFTING

Solution on page 247

Words about Words

```
E S A R H P R A M M A R G S
C W R I T I N G E N O U N J
D C O L O N O V E O Q O I S
F O R M A T I O N I I T L R
L J I A H T T A R T I C L E
A P N R C T C T S I S E E N
N R O E E V N E S S D J P I
G E J X E P U N A O R B S M
U D T R P Q J S L P O U B R
A I B F S N N E C E W S R E
G C Y G O L O H P R O M N T
E A Q D E S C R I P T I V E
S T O R Y R A N O I T C I D
Q E R U T C U R T S E L U R
```

ADJECTIVE	MORPHOLOGY	STRUCTURE
ARTICLE	NOUN	SUBJECT
CLASS	PERIOD	TENSE
COLON	PHRASE	TEXT
CONJUNCTION	PREDICATE	VERB
DESCRIPTIVE	PREPOSITION	WORDS
DETERMINERS	QUESTIONS	WRITING
DICTIONARY	RULES	
FORMATION	SPEECH	
GRAMMAR	SPELLING	
LANGUAGE	STORY	

Solution on page 247

Eat a Sandwich

```
H R E G R U B I M A L A S D
L E E L G O D T O H T P L A
E O R T L S U B M A R I N E
F I E O J A L G V O V E P R
A L G M L E B O U E W G P B
L N A A T L C T R R T G C P
A E S T O A S W A L L S U A
F K U O D H U P B E E A C S
R C A O D R A T S U M L U T
E I S E S I A N N O Y A M R
U H S T U C D L O C T D B A
B C L U B K F A O L T A E M
E J A M F D O O W G A D R I
N O C A B I N I N A P H A M
```

AVOCADO	DAGWOOD	MAYONNAISE	ROLL
BACON	EGG SALAD	MEATBALL	SALAMI
BLT	FALAFEL	MEATLOAF	SAUSAGE
BOLOGNA	HAM	MUSTARD	SPROUTS
BREAD	HERO	OIL	SUBMARINE
BURGER	HOAGIE	PANINI	TOMATO
CHICKEN	HOT DOG	PASTRAMI	WRAP
CLUB	JAM	PATTY MELT	
COLD CUTS	LETTUCE	PITA	
CUCUMBER	LIVERWURST	REUBEN	

Solution on page 248

Around the Ocean

```
L A K E M A R I N E L I F E
S W I M M I N G Y A D R F N
P I B S O N B K R N E D I V
A L I E P R C O A T O N S I
C D R V O O C L A C A E H R
I L D A R F S W K T H S I O
F I S W T I T E N C I A N N
I F E N I L T S A O C N G M
C E A D A A A E B G I D G E
I R S S M C B N F L U G W N
T I H R E S O R T P Z L E T
I V O Q D O L P H I N S L R
E E R O S I O N A E C O F S
S R E D I S A E S F F I L C
```

ATLANTIC	DOCK	PACIFIC	SEASIDE
BANK	DOLPHINS	PORT	SWIMMING
BEACHES	ENVIRONMENT	REGION	TAN
BIRDS	EROSION	RESORT	WAVES
BOATING	FISHING	RIVER	WILDLIFE
CALIFORNIA	GULF	ROCKY	
CITIES	ISLAND	SALT WATER	
CLIFFS	LAKE	SAND	
COASTLINE	MARINE LIFE	SEAGULLS	
CORAL	OCEAN	SEASHORE	

Solution on page 248

Cup of Coffee

```
T R J R J N E V G N O R T S
O E V B S I P N A D N E L B
P C M P L G N S I N G G P K
W U I R U A F S U H I U P J
O A L F U R C J T G C L M A
L S D R I O Y K G A A A L V
L I D E W M G S F P N R M A
A G N S R A B F F I L T E R
W D N H E T E V E E L S T O
S E A I D I A C L E R A M V
Y C Y R N C N R R E S N H A
S I I E I R S E T T J O R L
D N U O R G O A Y H T O R F
K Q C N G Y W M O C H A E F
```

AROMATIC	FRESH	JOE	SIP
BEANS	FRIENDS	LID	SLEEVE
BLACK	FROTHY	MACHINE	STRONG
BLEND	GOURMET	MILD	SUGAR
CAFFEINE	GRINDER	MOCHA	SWALLOW
CREAM	GROUND	MORNING	SYRUP
CUP	HOT	MUG	TASTY
DRINK	ICED	POT	VANILLA
FILTER	INSTANT	REGULAR	WATER
FLAVOR	JAVA	SAUCER	

Solution on page 248

Build a Rocket

```
Y B B O H R E P A P O G E E
T M I S C G N I Y L F U N D
E O E R Y S H O O T I Y E U
F D T E R C O N S T R U C T
A E U T T A I M N E E D A I
S L H E E L N E V N C O P T
K A C M K E M O G G G O S L
Y U A I C Y C I I L N W N A
B N R T O E N O I T C E J E
U C A L R E R D F L I G H T
I H P A S S E M B L Y N H S
L E X P L O S I V E S K G N
D R E M A E R T S U R H T I
D E E P S V C I T S A L P F
```

AIM	EXPLOSIVE	MODEL	SKY
ALTIMETERS	FINS	NOSE CONE	SPACE
ALTITUDE	FIRE	PAPER	SPEED
APOGEE	FLIGHT	PARACHUTE	STREAMER
ASSEMBLY	FLYING	PLASTIC	THRUST
BUILD	FUN	RECOVERY	WOOD
CONSTRUCT	GLIDE	ROCKETRY	
DEPLOYMENT	HOBBY	SAFETY	
EJECTION	IGNITION	SCALE	
ENGINES	LAUNCHER	SHOOT	

Solution on page 248

Cold Remedies

```
Z T H Y D R A T I O N X V T
S T N E M E L P P U S T A N
Z I N C A P S U L E S S P A
B R O T H T F O C G U E O L
Y T I V I T I S O P T R R A
R O T C O D L N U P P E I H
B L A N K E T S G E Y I Z N
G P X D E E H O H P L F E I
I E A P A G O A D P A I R G
N F L U I D S K R E C D L A
S T E L B A T W O R U I L R
E T R O F M O C P S E M I G
N L O Z E N G E S Y R U P L
G K U V Y A E C A N I H C E
```

BLANKETS	GARGLE	PILL	TABLET
BROTH	GINSENG	POSITIVITY	TEA
CAPSULES	GOOD BOOK	RELAXATION	VAPORIZER
COMFORT	HEATING PAD	REST	ZINC
COUGH DROP	HUMIDIFIER	SLEEP	
DOCTOR	HYDRATION	SOAK	
ECHINACEA	INHALANT	SOUP	
EUCALYPTUS	LOZENGES	SUPPLEMENTS	
FLUIDS	PEPPERS	SYRUP	

Solution on page 249

Puzzles

```
M B O X P C C H E S S D M C
E X E R C I S E Z Z I U Q R
L Y D X D I C E L D D I R I
B R I O N A H T R I V I A B
O T F I G U R E O F U N M B
R E F P I E C E S G N A E A
P M I N D B E N D E R W M G
E O C V X T O J D G I A H E
N E U I E I I D O L Z N M H
C G L S S G I T D E O A B T
I F T U S H P E E N I G M A
L Q L A B Y R I N T H R I M
T L W L R G A M E N T A L C
I P I C T U R E R E B M U N
```

ANAGRAM	FIGURE	LABYRINTH	PICTURE
BEWILDER	FINISH	LOGIC	PIECES
BOX	FUN	MATH	PROBLEM
CHESS	GAME	MAZE	QUIZZES
CRIBBAGE	GEOMETRY	MENTAL	RIDDLE
CRYPTOGRAM	HANOI	MINDBENDER	TEST
DIFFICULT	HIDDEN	NUMBER	TRIVIA
ENIGMA	ILLUSIONS	PENCIL	VISUAL
EXERCISE	JIGSAW	PICTOGRAM	

Solution on page 249

Catalogs

```
Y S C O I T E M S P O R T S
X I E L R E T A D P U P H A
M M N G O G F A S H I O N V
T R O D A T A B A S E L L I
T R E D E P H N K K F L Y N
E E E V E X D I I H R T A G
T D L G I L E D N Z E S R S
R R Y Y I L S D M G E O T I
Y O A N T S E S R U O C R Z
L B G G A S T D B Y S Y O E
I N B O W P E R U T C I P S
A E M O H P M O Y P R I C E
M W R D H P R O D U C T V O
J B T S I L T T C I P E D H
```

ART	FREE	MODELS	REGISTRY
BROWSE	GOODS	MUSIC	SALE
CLOTHING	HANDLING	NEW	SAVINGS
COMPANY	HOBBY	ORDER	SELL
COST	HOME	ORGANIZE	SHOE
COURSES	INDEXED	PAGES	SIZES
DATABASE	ITEMS	PICTURE	SPORTS
DELIVER	KIDS	PORTRAY	STYLE
DEPICT	LIST	PRICE	TOY
FASHION	MAIL	PRODUCT	UPDATE

Solution on page 249

Bouncy

```
A E M O T I O N I T A L E G N
N L L A B R N E R D L I H C
I A D S S E R T T A M V E O
M S A I S U H T N E J E N I
A T M O V E M E N T B L I L
T I B A B I E S Y K N I L S
E C J T S A N M Y G Z N O O
D E B U N N Y G R E N E P C
N I N F L A T A B L E S M C
U T E K R A M K C O T S A E
O G O P C U R L Y H A I R R
B S P R I N G N I S I R T I
E Z V F L I P U T T Y B D T
R A F T O Y S X J U M P O H
```

ANIMATED

BABIES

BALL

BED

BUNNY

CHILDREN

COILS

CURLY HAIR

DIVING BOARD

ELASTIC

ENERGY

ENTHUSIASM

FLIP

GELATIN

GYMNAST

HOP

INFLATABLE

JUMP

LIVELINESS

MATTRESS

MOTION

MOVEMENT

POGO

PUTTY

RAFT

REBOUND

RISING

SLINKY

SOCCER

SPRING

STOCK MARKET

TIRE

TOYS

TRAMPOLINE

Solution on page 249

Hire Some Help

```
K R O W U S E F U L P G G D
H S W E R C S S L I A N E R
A E P R O J E C T S I I M I
M R S B O J D D O L N B O L
M V K R F T L G E A T M H L
E I A I I I C D G C I U E L
R C E N U A O A O I N L L A
O E L B B M P N R R G P P W
I L I C E N S E D T O W F Y
R O I R E T X E R C N O U R
E C G B R H O U S E H O L D
T E A U P S K I L L E D C F
N M C L H C A R P E N T R Y
I T O O L B O X F I X I N G
```

BUILD	FLOOR	PAINTING	USEFUL
CALL	HAMMER	PLUMBING	VAN
CARPENTRY	HELPFUL	PROJECTS	WOOD
CONSTRUCT	HOME	REMODELING	WORK
CONTRACTOR	HOUSEHOLD	REPAIRS	
DRILL	INTERIOR	ROOF	
DRYWALL	LEAKS	SCREWS	
ELECTRICAL	LICENSED	SERVICE	
EXTERIOR	NAILS	SKILLED	
FIXING	ODD JOBS	TOOLBOX	

Solution on page 250

Festivals

```
N W O T E K C I T Y F O L K
J S C H I L D R E N J E S F
S U D O O F A M I L Y U T E
U C B L H A R V E S T C S A
M R K I D A N C I N G E E S
M I I D L W I N E N M B T T
E C P A G E A N T U R R N R
R O G Y F I E S T A R A O E
T U B S P O N S O R S B C E
S N V E N D O R S H M C D T
W T E A E C U L T U R A L J
O Y R V A R F O S P R I N G
H T C K E U O I G A M E S X
S P E N N B C U P F I L M M
```

ARTS	COSTUMES	FOLK	PARADE
BARBECUE	COUNTY	FOOD	SHOWS
BEER	CULTURAL	FUN	SPONSOR
BOOTHS	DANCING	GALA	SPRING
CAKE	EVENT	GAMES	STREET
CARNIVAL	FAIR	HARVEST	SUMMER
CHILDREN	FAMILY	HOLIDAY	TICKET
CIRCUS	FEAST	JUBILEE	TOWN
CITY	FIESTA	MUSIC	VENDORS
CONTESTS	FILM	PAGEANT	WINE

Solution on page 250

Comfort Food

```
Y M A E R C G N I D D U P G
A B R O W N I E S B U B A N
M M E A T B A L L S M A T I
S F G S H C H I L I P C S F
N R R T A A M E A T L O A F
O I U R N N M F R S I N P U
O E B A K E D B E A N S D T
D S E K A C G W U O G E E S
L A S A G N A L I R S U S E
E S E I K O O C U C G L S L
S G E L A T I N L D H E E F
O T H I S O O T H I N G R F
D P C S P A G H E T T I T A
A E T B R E A D S L L O R W
```

BACON	CREAMY	MEATBALLS	SODA
BAKED BEANS	DESSERT	MEATLOAF	SOOTHING
BREADS	DUMPLINGS	NOODLES	SPAGHETTI
BROWNIES	FRIES	PASTA	STUFFING
CAKE	GELATIN	PIE	SUGAR
CARBS	HAMBURGER	PUDDING	TEA
CHEESEBURGER	HOT	ROAST	WAFFLES
CHILI	INDULGENT	ROLLS	YAMS
COOKIES	LASAGNA	SANDWICH	

Solution on page 250

First Date

```
Y J I T T E R S U O V R E N
F U N A F F E C T I O N F F
G G I J A W K W A R D O L Y
N N G T S E R E T N I I O H
I I H N F L U T T E R S W S
H N T D I N N E R T T S E N
G R B L I N D D A T E E R O
U A D A N C E T C E N R S I
A E I V O M I V T E S P I T
L L E B R O O D I M I M L S
Y N E W N E S S O L O I L E
H O E B E G I N N I N G Y U
U E C S U O V Z E D N E R Q
G N I L W O B D E T I C X E
```

AFFECTION	DINNER	IMPRESSION	NIGHT
ATTRACTION	DOORBELL	INTEREST	QUESTIONS
AWKWARD	ENLIVENING	JITTERS	RENDEZVOUS
BEGINNING	EXCITED	LAUGHING	SHY
BLIND DATE	FLIRTATION	LEARNING	SILLY
BOWLING	FLOWERS	MEET	TENSION
CAR	FLUTTER	MOVIE	
COY	FUN	NERVOUS	
DANCE	HUG	NEWNESS	

Solution on page 250

Fall

```
A J D L O O H C S D U O L C
U H U N T I N G H I X V B R
T S R O I B R A N C H E S I
U O P E R W T T I K J R R S
M F R O D S J H K C T C O P
N I W A R I A E P A S A L X
F N T F N C C R M T E S O J
E I R T O G K I U S V T C H
A E E O E O E N P Y R O O S
S Z G L C N T G X A A O A A
T I N L D S S B K H H B T U
R A A I E S W E A T E R S Q
A M H H D R U O G L O V E S
W H C C Q S E V A E L P P A
```

APPLE	COATS	GOURD	OVERCAST
AUTUMN	COLORS	HARVEST	PUMPKIN
BOOTS	CORN	HATS	RAKE
BRANCHES	CRISP	HAYSTACK	SCHOOL
BROWN	CROPS	HUNTING	SQUASH
CHANGE	FEAST	JACKETS	STRAW
CHESTNUTS	FIELD	LEAVES	SWEATERS
CHILL	FOOTBALL	MAIZE	WIND
CIDER	GATHERING	MITTENS	
CLOUDS	GLOVES	ORANGE	

Solution on page 251

34

Backyard

```
E D A H S T O N E X A L E R
A R B O R E W O L F E D C Y
L T W E E S T E P U I G N T
W L E D H J N E D R A G E R
K C I R B N I A T N U O F A
D L U R R E L K N I R P S P
S B D O G A H K B T X E E T
S O I T A P C A J U O Y M A
A O R R I E R E I R B A A B
R B I R D H O U S E D W G L
G E A O I B P L A Y N K A E
Z Z H O S E A S O N A L T K
O A C E D I S T U O S A E A
S G K C O M M A H L P W U R
```

ARBOR	FOUNTAIN	OUTSIDE	SEASONAL
BIRDBATH	FURNITURE	PARTY	SHADE
BIRDHOUSE	GAMES	PATIO	SHRUBS
BRICK	GARDEN	PETS	SLIDE
CHAIR	GATE	PLAY	SPRINKLER
DECK	GAZEBO	POOL	STONE
DIRT	GRASS	PORCH	TABLE
DOG	GRILL	RAKE	TERRACE
FENCE	HAMMOCK	RELAX	TREE
FLOWER	HOSE	SANDBOX	WALKWAY

Solution on page 251

Baby Products

```
F O R M U L A T L O T I O N
M D R E S S E R E I R R A C
C E G N I D D E B K U C E G
R L B I B F B R H X N H B T
E T S Y O T I O O P M A H S
A T A E S R A C D C B N L L
M O C R A D L E A Y K G R B
A B D I A P E R S P W E A C
T A M Y A L P E K H L A R M
T E N I S S A B C L T I S S
R E L B A T L I O Y B A B H
E B O U N C E R S K O O B O
S H M O N I T O R A T T L E
S T E E H S E H T O L C W S
```

BABY OIL	BOTTLE	DIAPERS	ROCKER
BABY SEAT	BOUNCER	DRESSER	SHAMPOO
BASSINET	CAR SEAT	FORMULA	SHEETS
BATH SEAT	CARRIER	LOTION	SHOES
BEDDING	CHANGE	MATTRESS	SOCKS
BIB	CLOTHES	MONITOR	STROLLER
BLANKET	CRADLE	PACIFIER	TABLE
BODYWASH	CREAM	PLAY MAT	TOYS
BOOKS	CRIB	RATTLE	

Solution on page 251

Psychiatric Therapy

```
H O S P I T A L N I A R B U
C Y Y G O L O H C Y S P E G
R R T M N I L L N E S S H U
A V E N E I H U M A N Y A I
E S C P E M L H C U O C V L
S N I I R M O E P L E H I T
E O F S D E P R E S S I O N
R I F Z Y E S O I F X A R E
D T O E D L A S L E F T O M
R O F A N T A S I E S R T T
E M P A T I E N T O V Y C A
A E A U S T R I A N N E O E
M I N D C H I L D H O O D R
S T U D Y P R O B L E M S T
```

ANALYSIS	DREAMS	ILLNESS	RESEARCH
AUSTRIAN	EMOTIONS	MEMORIES	STUDY
BEHAVIOR	FANTASIES	MIND	TREATMENT
BRAIN	FEELINGS	OFFICE	
CHILDHOOD	GUILT	PATIENT	
COUCH	HELP	PROBLEMS	
DEPRESSION	HOSPITAL	PSYCHIATRY	
DEVELOPMENT	HUMAN	PSYCHOLOGY	
DOCTOR	IDEAS	REPRESSION	

Solution on page 251

Breakfast Food

```
S E I R R E B W A R T S U S
A L M I L K F Y O G U R T E
U B L U E B E R R I E S S G
S J O O A Q A T U T M E T D
A S X P R N U A C I E G I I
G E P H G N K I N H T G U R
E L E E F F O C C A U S C R
E F N O C A B M A H N P S O
B F R I T T A T A T E A I P
A A E M S E K A C N A P B A
G W E C R O I S S A N T I S
E A J C I S M O O T H I E T
L N I F F U M L A E R E C R
N J E L L Y J A M G R A V Y
```

APPLE	CROISSANT	LOX	SMOOTHIE
BACON	EGGS	MILK	STRAWBERRIES
BAGEL	FRITTATA	MUFFIN	TEA
BANANA	FRUIT	OATMEAL	WAFFLES
BISCUITS	GRAVY	ORANGE	YOGURT
BLUEBERRIES	HAM	PANCAKES	
CEREAL	JAM	PASTRY	
CINNAMON ROLLS	JELLY	PORRIDGE	
COFFEE	JUICE	QUICHE	
CREAM CHEESE	KETCHUP	SAUSAGE	

Solution on page 252

Industrial

```
B U S I N E S S E N I G N E
P G N I D L I U B S P E E D
O S M N E M P L O Y M E N T
L E W D T L A B O R C E B B
L N A U A U E Q S A V M S I
U I R S M M Y C L I H E T C
T H E T O B L I T T C C N O
I C H R T E B O G R M H E M
O A O Y U R M N U E O A M M
N M U F A O E O K G D N P E
O D S T T R S I C N E I I R
R U E U T E S N U A R C U C
I O A S R F A U R D N A Q E
G L O V E S D E T A I L E D
```

ASSEMBLY	EMPLOYMENT	MECHANICAL
AUTOMATED	ENGINES	MODERN
AUTOMOTIVE	EQUIPMENT	POLLUTION
BUILDING	GLOVES	RESOURCES
BUSINESS	INDUSTRY	SPEED
CALIBRATE	IRON	STRENGTH
COMMERCE	LABOR	TRUCK
DANGER	LOUD	UNION
DETAILED	LUMBER	WAREHOUSE
ELECTRONIC	MACHINES	

Solution on page 252

Global Geography

```
H N P A I N K S E I T I C M
T Y O F U D N A L S I K S A
R R P R Y S B C N E B E C I
A T U I T S T I U V S I G N
E N L C X H A R G S T A E L
B U A A T T A E A C F N O A
O O T F N S O M R L S S L N
U C I U I G D A E A I N O D
N R O A R N T H L R S A G I
D M N A A N S T O G I E I V
A I P L A O A U J E N C C I
R H S R E D R O B O D O A D
Y F D S N O I S I V I D L E
E B O L G R E E N L A N D D
```

AFRICA	CITIES	GEOLOGICAL	MOUNTAINS
AMERICAS	COUNTRY	GLOBE	NORTH AMERICA
ANTARCTICA	DIVIDED	GREENLAND	OCEANS
AREAS	DIVISIONS	INDIA	POPULATION
ATLAS	DRIFT	ISLAND	SHELF
AUSTRALIA	EARTH	LANDMASSES	SOUTH AMERICA
BORDERS	EURASIA	LARGE	
BOUNDARY	GEOGRAPHY	MAINLAND	

Solution on page 252

Tennis Player

```
T S U E J D R O P S H O T G
J A R Y U R R O D L A V E R
S N E E S T A N S M I T H E
O D K L T R U O C K C A B B
R R C L I S E G D U B N O D
R E E A N T J F A U L T H E
A A B N E D L I T L L I B N
G G S L H B A L L B O Y W A
D A I Y E L L O V C Q I T F
N S R O N N O C Y M M I J E
A S O M I D C O U R T I B T
L I B E N I L E S A B J K S
O M I C H A E L C H A N G S
R E R E D E F R E G O R A H
```

ALLEY	DROP SHOT	MIDCOURT
ANDRE AGASSI	FAULT	ROD LAVER
BACKCOURT	ITF	ROGER FEDERER
BALL BOY	JIMMY CONNORS	ROLAND GARROS
BASELINE	JUSTINE HENIN	STAN SMITH
BILL TILDEN	KIM CLIJSTERS	STEFAN EDBERG
BORIS BECKER	LET	VOLLEY
DON BUDGE	MICHAEL CHANG	

Solution on page 252`

Political Life

```
J X Q P Y T I R O J A M F E
O T A R C O M E D P U O R G
P O W E R E V O L U T I O N
U T N S Y T I R O H T U A A
S N O I S I C E D N E I M H
N A I D H O U S E T C I C C
O T T E T N E M A I L R A P
I I P N L X N R T I L C M L
T O U T A R O I T A A E P A
C N R T E P L A W D R T A T
E A R V R O R S E W E A I F
L L O O P Y X M G K D T G O
E G C A N D I D A T E S N R
E V I T U C E X E K F M S M
```

ACADEMIC	EXECUTIVE	PLATFORM
AUTHORITY	FEDERAL	POLITICIAN
CAMPAIGNS	GOVERNMENT	POWER
CANDIDATES	GROUP	PRESIDENT
CHANGE	HOUSE	REVOLUTION
CORPORATE	LAWS	STATE
CORRUPTION	MAJORITY	TAXES
DECISIONS	MILITARY	
DEMOCRAT	NATIONAL	
ELECTIONS	PARLIAMENT	

Solution on page 253

Art History

```
S L G E S N G I S E D Q L P
K A E R N E G N T E V R A C
E Y V N R E A L I S M D R I
T E T N E I C N A T O A U A
C R A D A R A S R Y N V M S
H S P R B C V C T L E I E O
P W A A E A U U R E T N A M
R F E W R P R T O Y O C S P
E R U I Y T M O P L L I E L
L A T N A T I E Q A R I L A
I M A G E S U S T U N U C U
E E T F O R M A T S E E W S
F T S A C V M U E S U M L I
W A R H O L F E L B R A M V
```

ACRYLIC

ANCIENT

ARTISTS

BAROQUE

BEAUTY

CANVAS

CARVE

CAST

CUT

DA VINCI

DESIGNS

DRAWING

EASEL

FORMATS

FRAME

FUTURISM

GENRE

IMAGES

LAYERS

LOUVRE

MARBLE

MONET

MOSAIC

MURAL

MUSEUM

OIL

PAINTING

PANEL

PORTRAIT

REALISM

RELIEF

SCENE

SKETCH

STATUE

STYLE

TEMPERA

VISUAL

WARHOL

Solution on page 253

On the Tube

```
S S L E N N A H C P B S C A
G K F A M I L Y G U Y E O W
N E R O D I G I T A L I L A
I L A O X A T H G S T V O R
T B N C W S N E A M I O R D
A A A B A T N T M R U M O S
R C L A C R E O E I P S V M
R N O X S L T N S N R O I O
E N G M L B M O H P N P V C
A U D I E N C E O N M A R T
L V T M E D I A W N P I U I
I E R P F R I E N D S S S S
T O B H D A T E L I N E E C
Y D L E F N I E S A M A R D
```

ABC	COLOR	GAME SHOW	PRIME TIME
ANALOG	COMEDIES	HBO	RATINGS
ANTENNA	CSI	MEDIA	REALITY
AUDIENCE	DATELINE	MOVIES	SATELLITE
AWARDS	DIGITAL	MTV	SEINFELD
CABLE	DRAMAS	MUSIC	SIMPSONS
CARTOONS	ESPN	NBC	SITCOMS
CBS	FAMILY GUY	NETWORKS	SURVIVOR
CHANNELS	FOX	OPRAH	
CNN	FRIENDS	PBS	

Solution on page 253

Sewing Supplies

```
E N I H C A M R E P P I Z L
L N I B B O B M O C R N G N
B D O U M Q E L T H E T R O
M M F T Q H Y I E A T E E T
I P A T T E R N M L T R P T
H O S T S U N E P K U F P O
T O T T E E B N L S C A I C
O H E S L R O C A U Y C R I
L R N D C T I E T M R I M R
C I E W I T M A E D A N A B
P E R O S E S I L K T G E A
N S N A P S C I S S O R S F
G S L A K C I T S D R A Y G
J E T L E F N O B B I R O N
```

BOBBIN	HOOP	PINS	TEMPLATE
BUTTON	INTERFACING	POLYESTER	THIMBLE
CHALK	IRON	RIBBON	YARDSTICK
CLOTH	LINEN	ROTARY CUTTER	ZIPPER
COTTON	MACHINE	RULER	
ELASTIC	MANNEQUIN	SCISSORS	
FABRIC	MATERIAL	SEAM RIPPER	
FASTENER	NEEDLE	SILK	
FELT	NOTIONS	SNAPS	
HEM	PATTERN	TAPE MEASURE	

Solution on page 253

Loud Music

```
Y W O H S X J D K C O R R R
E G E L L O C E L Y P E J E
O S T A E B S A M B S P A I
G B U L C M M F R O T O Z F
N E N B N O U E U T N U Z I
I C N O R O R N O H E N N L
B N A O X B D I E E L D E P
B A U N H I W N R R U I I M
O S N P N P O G E S B N G A
R I O G O O O U T O R G H Y
H U I C K L Y R S M U E B T
T N S S A B I I C E T D O R
L I E C N A D C N I J U R A
D S G U L P R A E G M R S P
```

AMPLIFIER

ANNOYING

BASS

BEATS

BOOM BOX

BOTHERSOME

CAR

CLAMOROUS

CLUB

COLLEGE

DANCE

DEAFENING

DISCO

DRUMS

EARPLUGS

INDUSTRIAL

JAZZ

MICROPHONE

NEIGHBORS

NOISE

NUISANCE

OBNOXIOUS

PARTY

POLICE

POUNDING

RAP

RESOUNDING

ROCK

RUDE

SHOWY

STEREO

THROBBING

TURBULENT

Solution on page 254

Casinos

```
O N I W G G H S A C K S I R
D N Y T R A P R U R P E C A
D Y E N O M D N E A T H L X
S E E K O E R Y R E I C E S
B L A C K J A C K P O T S R
I F L U I L C N S H N T E E
N F O L P D U X O A A L F S
G U S Y O J E L S B A V E O
O H I D K R O U L E T T E L
E S N A E B K E D T N E V E
D V G L R T G N I K N I R D
I M I N I M U M A X I M U M
V F F O Y A P I T B O S S I
D T O L S W A G E R F U N G
```

ALCOHOL	CRAPS	LADY LUCK	PLAYER
ANTE	DEALER	LOSERS	POKER
BANKROLL	DICE	LOSING	RISK
BET	DRINKING	MAXIMUM	ROULETTE
BINGO	EVENT	MINIMUM	SHUFFLE
BLACKJACK	FUN	MONEY	SLOT
CARD	GAME	ODDS	TABLE
CASH	JACKPOTS	PARTY	VIDEO
CHIPS	JUNKET	PAYOFF	WAGER
COMPS	KENO	PIT BOSS	WIN

Solution on page 254

Travel Abroad

```
W X A L E R U T L U C S R S
F A L E N A L P T E K N U J
J Z L T I C K E T S T Y O B
P A C K S M O T S U C S T F
L O D G I N G Y E N R U O J
T O P N U N E E E P I R T H
R R B I C L G G S L E T O H
O E O P H O A R A I L W A Y
P G R P A S U V G G U I D E
R A D O S T G N I N G R D T
I L E H I S N P T R I U C A
A L R S L E A R N R R Y L X
J I I E R O L P X E Y A L I
X V Y A W B U S T H G I S F
```

AGENCY	EXPLORE	LODGING	SUBWAY
AIRPORT	FLYING	LUGGAGE	TAXI
ARRIVAL	FOREIGN	PACK	TICKETS
BORDER	GUIDE	PASSPORT	TOUR
BUS	HOSTEL	PLANE	TRIP
COUNTRY	HOTEL	RAILWAY	VILLAGE
CRUISE	JOURNEY	RELAX	VISIT
CUISINE	JUNKET	SHIP	WALKING
CULTURE	LANGUAGE	SHOPPING	
CUSTOMS	LEARN	SIGHTS	

Solution on page 254

Going Shopping

```
S C E R O T S E O H S R A W
L N S T A T I O N E R Y R O
A S I S N P R I C E L E O R
E G R A H C P N E T T S T R
D D O N G T A L L D K W A O
E L E C T R O N I C S O L B
B G G H A U A R B A V R A E
I R N E R O E B O O N B C R
T O L C E C I G M R Y C S O
C C L K T D K I O S K B E T
A E O O A O R E T U R N S S
R R R U I O C O U P O N S T
D Y T T L F R H A G G L E E
C Z S K C E H C K N A B N P
```

APPLIANCES

AUTOMOBILE

BABY STORE

BANK CHECK

BARGAINS

BORROW

BROWSE

CHARGE

CHECKOUT

CLEARANCES

COUPONS

DEALS

DEBIT CARD

DIRECTORY

ELECTRONICS

ESCALATOR

FOOD COURT

GROCERY

HAGGLE

KIOSK

LOAN

PET STORE

PRICE

RETAIL

RETURNS

SHOE STORE

STATIONERY

STROLL

Solution on page 254

Geological Study

```
A S E N O T S L I S S O F H
T L C D T H A P E L T N A M
A A I I C I N O T C E T U I
R R M U Q S D S R E Y A L N
T E S Q M T S C O N G C T I
S N I I A O T R C O R E S N
I I E L P R O U K Y O D I G
G M S N P Y N S S G U C G S
O S L A I R E T A M N L N E
L M O U N T A I N S D I E T
O S M E G L N A M G A M O A
E L I O S D O O L F P A U L
G A M B E R U T C U R T S P
S O L I D N O I S O R E A Z
```

AMBER	FLOODS	MAGMA	SANDSTONE
CLIMATE	FOSSILS	MANTLE	SEISMIC
CONTINENT	GEMS	MAPPING	SOIL
CORE	GEOLOGIST	MATERIALS	SOLID
CRUST	GROUND	MINERALS	STONES
CRYSTALS	HISTORY	MINING	STRATA
DIRT	IGNEOUS	MOUNTAINS	STRUCTURE
EROSION	LAYERS	PLATES	TECTONIC
FAULTS	LIQUID	ROCKS	TIME

Solution on page 255

Happy Anniversary

```
S P E C I A L H A R M O N Y
F R I E N D S R E W O L F L
V Y S F M I H U S R A E Y S
B D G A R U E T R T W G E Y
O N U E S C N D H P I I L R
N A H B N E X I N F R I F L
D C A A S S A Y T O M I G E
E N M E Z N N S M A M O S W
D O R G N O L E F I L A D E
R P C U M O M V Q D O P I J
E B A E E L I B U J V A N D
K L R H O L I D A Y E R N A
A E D E G A I R R A M T E T
C C E L E B R A T E L Y R E
```

ANNUAL	DATE	HOLIDAY	PARTY
BALLOONS	DIAMOND	HUGS	PLATINUM
BONDED	DINNER	HUSBAND	PRESENTS
CAKE	FAMILY	JEWELRY	ROMANCE
CANDY	FLOWERS	JUBILEE	SPECIAL
CARD	FRIENDS	LIFELONG	SURPRISE
CELEBRATE	GIFTS	LOVE	WIFE
CEREMONY	GOLD	MARRIAGE	YEARS
CHERISH	HARMONY	MEMORIES	

Solution on page 255

Housecleaning

```
V T W I P E L A T H E R K T
M A O T O I L E T H T O L C
A Z C W J V K S D U S T F B
E J G U E C E G S C R U B Y
L P O M U L A L A U N D R Y
G Y I B K M S O K R A S O B
X R K M L P P V K R B O O U
G C R A O E R E I K A A M S
S C A N E O A S T L S P G B
P L G W O U R C C E G D S E
R E S L X I Q D H T L I F W
A A F R U O C S E L B B U B
Y N W E D L I M N B U F F O
R E T A W D E N I H S A W C
```

BEDROOM	DUST	MOP	SWEEP
BLEACH	FILTH	RAGS	TOILET
BROOM	FLOOR	SCOUR	TOWELS
BRUSH	GARBAGE	SCRUB	VACUUM
BUBBLES	GLEAM	SHINE	WASH
BUCKET	GLOVES	SOAP	WATER
BUFF	GRIME	SPARKLE	WIPE
CLEAN	KITCHEN	SPONGE	
CLOTH	LATHER	SPRAY	
COBWEBS	LAUNDRY	SQUEAKY	
DISHES	MILDEW	SUDS	

Solution on page 255

Fashion Design

```
K R S D E S I G N E M O W D
L T O B U Y E R S K E T C H
A A C L Q J E W E L R Y E W
W I I T O T L F B E A U T Y
T L A R T C A F M S E N A L
A O L A E B U U U G N I E E
C R P Y R T S U D N I Q R B
T C H I C N A F R I Z U C A
R U C S O A C M E W A E L L
I T N C U I T O S A G J O V
K A E H T L R D S R A W T F
S H R O U A E E M D M Z H C
G K F O R T N L S H O E S J
S T Y L E I D E A S T N A P
```

ART	CUT	JEWELRY	SKIRT
BEAUTY	DESIGN	LABEL	SOCIAL
BUYERS	DRAWING	MAGAZINE	STYLE
CASUAL	DRESS	MATERIAL	TAILOR
CATWALK	FABRIC	MODEL	TREND
CHIC	FRENCH	PANTS	UNIQUE
CLOTH	FUN	PATTERN	WOMEN
COLOR	HAT	SCHOOL	
CONSUMER	IDEAS	SEW	
COUTURE	INDUSTRY	SHOES	
CREATE	ITALIAN	SKETCH	

Solution on page 255

Travel by Train

```
W X C R A I L W A Y S T N G
D X O A S T A T I O N I Q C
I R A C L I A R S E A T S O
E M L G E S R A C R M E Y N
S O D N E N I L T P L V E D
E N V I W A G R C A L I X U
L O K N S R E I E S U T P C
E R A I L T R A N S P O R T
C A R D U D A L N E U M E O
T I T M H I K N O N B O S R
R L M T O P E D C G L C S T
I O A T R A V E L E I O L E
C S D A O R L I A R C L N M
S T E A M G N I S S O R C G
```

AMTRAK	ELECTRIC	RAIL TRANSPORT
CARS	ENGINE	RAILCAR
COAL	EXPRESS	RAILROADS
COMMUTER TRAIN	LINE	RAILWAYS
CONDUCTOR	LOCOMOTIVE	RAPID TRANSIT
CONNECT	LONG	SEATS
CROSSING	METRO	STATION
DEPOT	MONORAIL	STEAM
DIESEL	PASSENGERS	TRAVEL
DINING CAR	PUBLIC	
DISTANCE	PULLMAN	

Solution on page 256

Play the Violin

```
V S H E E T M U S I C I A N
S C V I N S T R U M E N T S
O I A C O U S T I C S Z X S
U N F E C N A M R O F R E P
N O A O G N I Y A L P T I C
D M R R U B A N V Z O T O E
I R T E L R O S I N C N E L
F A S L L S S E D H C B G L
F H E D O M S T A E C A D O
I B H D R A O B R E G N I F
C O C I C L L T T I T D R N
U W R F S L O R S Y N O B E
L U O T U N I N G P E G S C
T E T R A U Q G N I R T S K
```

ACOUSTICS	DIFFICULT	NECK	SHEET MUSIC
BAND	EBONY	NOTES	SMALL
BOW	FIDDLER	ORCHESTRA	SOLO
BRIDGE	FINGERBOARD	PERFORMANCE	SOUND
CASE	FOUR STRINGS	PITCH	STRADIVARIUS
CELLO	HARMONICS	PLAYING	STRING QUARTET
CHIN	INSTRUMENTS	ROSIN	TUNING PEGS
CONCERTO	MUSICIAN	SCROLL	

Solution on page 256

Gleeful

```
E J K H U P L I F T E D E G
L U F H T R I M E R R Y L T
G I D E T H G I L E D A K N
G L G N I M A E B X D G C A
I U C H E E R Y F H E S U Y
G F E N T E R T A I N A H O
R E G N I H G U A L D T C U
D E Y O J R E V O A E I J B
E L P Y T N U A J R T S O J
S G Y P P A H Y R A A F V O
A J U B I L A N T T L I I Y
E N I R G H A S J E E E A O
L F R O L I C Y S D Z D L U
P D A N C E U P H O R I C S
```

BEAMING	ELATED	GLEEFUL	LIGHTHEARTED
BUOYANT	ENTERTAIN	GRIN	MERRY
CHEERY	EUPHORIC	HAPPY	MIRTHFUL
CHIPPER	EXHILARATED	JAUNTY	OVERJOYED
CHUCKLE	FROLIC	JOVIAL	PLAY
DANCE	GAY	JOYOUS	PLEASED
DELIGHTED	GIGGLE	JUBILANT	SATISFIED
ECSTATIC	GLAD	LAUGHING	UPLIFTED

Solution on page 256

Urban Living

```
S D W O R C O M M U T E R B
R S S V I P A U K T S E D Y
I K Y T O I N A O T T E A C
A Y Y L R I N W O T N W O D
T S I P C E N R I S E N E E
S C O I P H E L E E D T L L
E R P S O S I T R O A E L P
T A A U L K G F S L V I S O
L P S B L R H R U A V X T E
E E T W U A B P T E B A U P
S R H A T P O O L O F T D D
I E G Y I P R Y A W H G I H
O N I G O M S E C I F F O U
N T L I N D U S T R Y Y D B
```

AIRPORT	FREEWAY	NOISE	STAIRS
BARS	HIGHWAY	OFFICES	STORES
BUS	HUB	PARKS	STREETS
CITY	INDUSTRY	PEOPLE	STUDIO
COMMUTE	LIGHTS	POLICE	SUBWAY
CONDOS	LITTER	POLLUTION	TAXI
CROWDS	LIVELY	POPULATED	TOWNHOUSES
DENSE	LOFT	RENT	
DOWNTOWN	MUNICIPAL	SKYSCRAPER	
ELEVATOR	NEIGHBORS	SMOG	

Solution on page 256

Museum Visit

```
U S C U L P T U R E D N O W
S R I N E V U O S A V N A C
S U R E F P I R T D L E I F
R A R T X N O S T A L G I A
E S K E T C H E N S S A P K
V O R C W W A O R Y E I K N
O N O N T F I V R U H U G O
C I T E H T S E A S T N G W
S D A I A A L S R T I A L L
I Z R C O L L E C T I O N E
D N U S A E B L N R U O T D
W D C G D M C I L E R A N G
E G B O E X A M I N I N G E
M U M M Y P A M P H L E T E
```

AESTHETIC
ART
CANVAS
COLLECTION
CURATOR
DINOSAURS
DISCOVER
EDUCATIONAL
EXAMINING
EXCAVATION

FIELD TRIP
GALLERY
GUEST
HALL
KNOWLEDGE
MEMBERSHIP
MODELS
MUMMY
NATURE
NOSTALGIA

PAINTING
PAMPHLET
PASS
RELIC
SCIENCE
SCULPTURE
SKETCH
SOUVENIRS
TOUR
WONDER

Solution on page 257

Mountain Climbing

```
S Y R A L L I H E I G H T S
K S A F E T Y D L E V A R T
I T E V E R E S T I B E T E
I I C E A X E N O N I R X E
N M A T H L E T I C E E P P
G M I Z A C R S A H R C A E
H U R P S A N L T C U L S B
I S E E I O G A I E T V A A
K N D N P N E S L I N S G P
I B I M I W E B T A E T E E
N N A P C D O U E C V D A A
G R M O I O D N A L D A R K
C A L U T E K M S C A V E S
C D G S A L P I N E G Y X O
```

ADVENTURE	CAVES	HIKING	SUMMITS
ALPINE	COLD	HILLARY	TENT
ALTITUDE	CRAMPONS	ICE AXE	TIBET
ASCENT	DESCENT	NEPAL	TRAINING
ATHLETIC	EVEREST	OXYGEN	TRAVEL
AVALANCHE	EXERCISE	PEAKS	WEATHER
BASE CAMP	GEAR	SAFETY	
BELAY	GLACIERS	SKIING	
BOOTS	GUIDE	SNOW	
CAMPING	HEIGHTS	STEEP	

Solution on page 257

Baking

```
O T I R I T S L V D A E R B
K V W V Y E A S T Z W Z O O
H R E V D B P E S N E A L W
R U E N G O E U B D K L L L
V O E R O R G L D G A G E H
V L H N U A G E P I C E R F
B F A A R S S N I F F U M F
Y N D Y M A A B R O W N Y T
C O O L E W C E T S A B J B
S E Z R T R D K M I H U A W
X S G S P W I A T A M A H A
G I U T O A F N E L E E P T
T R M P I H W A G N A R R E
C U P Y V Q Z P L T K S C R
```

APRON	CUP	MUFFINS	SPOON
BASTE	EGGS	OVEN	STIR
BEAT	FLOUR	PAN	SUGAR
BLEND	GLAZE	POWDER	TIMER
BOWL	GOURMET	RACK	WATER
BREAD	GREASED	RECIPE	WHIP
BROWN	HEAT	RISE	YEAST
CAKE	KNEAD	ROLLER	
COOL	LAYERING	SALT	
CREAM	MEASURE	SHAPE	
CRUST	MIX	SODA	

Solution on page 257

Managers at Work

```
T I U S T E A M W O R K D C
C L E E H W G I B F E P A Y
E O O T X B U S Y I Y R E E
R T A R A E E V T R O O V E
I N G C T R C T N I L J A S
D E Y N H N O U A N P E L R
F G M Y I H O P T G M C U E
O A U O L T E C R I E T A V
R E E I N D E L O O V L T O
E B S U D I N E P I C E E D
M O T I V A T E M F Y T U D
A S Q Y A S N O I T U L O S
N S R E E R A C R R P L A N
U O R G A N I Z E T F I H S
```

AGENT	EMPLOYER	MOTIVATE
BIG WHEEL	EVALUATE	ORGANIZE
BOSS	EXECUTIVE	OVERSEE
BUSY	FIRING	PAY
CAREER	FOREMAN	PLAN
COACH	FRIENDLY	PROJECT
CONTROL	GUIDANCE	RAISE
CORPORATE	HELPFUL	SHIFT
DELEGATE	IMPORTANT	SOLUTIONS
DIRECT	MEETING	SUIT
DUTY	MONITOR	TEAMWORK

Solution on page 257

Flower Shop

```
Y S I A D I H C R O L N P S
B O U Q U E T U L I P S U L
D E K C I P C T D A S I R L
N G G S B L O O M I N G C E
W R E A T H F A R V B O H M
M W H R N F R I F A R Y A S
A B Y F A Y I L N S T R S L
I L A D L N O G A E I E E I
N O C L P R I G B G Y V S L
U S I R I S E U O G P I O I
T S N S E V O L M Q R L R E
E O T D Q T D F L O W E R S
P M H B O W S G N I D D E W
S L A T E P G A R L A N D N
```

AMARYLLIS	DECORATE	IRIS	ROSES
ASTER	DELIVERY	LILIES	SMELLS
BLOOMING	DESIGN	LOVE	TULIPS
BLOSSOM	FLORIST	MARIGOLD	VASE
BOUQUET	FLOWERS	ORCHID	WEDDINGS
BOWS	GARLAND	PETALS	WREATH
CORSAGE	GERANIUM	PETUNIA	
CUT	GIFTS	PICKED	
DAFFODIL	GREEN	PLANT	
DAISY	HYACINTH	PURCHASE	

Solution on page 258

Autographs

```
B Y T R A D E L J E R S E Y
W A H O U N D T S I T R A N
R H N S T A R H O C K E Y E
I B P D H T E K C I T Y B P
T O K A O C B A S E B A L L
E O F O R G E R Y L S L T E
U K F J O G H L H K A P A T
L L A B T O O F E A S C T T
A N M F C L B T R B T O H E
V A O W E F B B O O R S L R
I M U B L A Y B R H O I E S
N E S L L I B Y A L P G T B
K U F L O U R I S H S N E Y
M U S I C I A N O I T C U A
```

ACTOR
ALBUM
ARTIST
ATHLETE
AUCTION
AUTHOR
BAND
BASEBALL
BASKETBALL
BOOK

CELEBRITY
COLLECTOR
COSIGN
FAKE
FAMOUS
FLOURISH
FOOTBALL
FORGERY
GOLF
HAT

HERO
HOBBY
HOCKEY
HOUND
INK
JERSEY
LETTERS
MUSICIAN
NAME
PEN

PHOTOGRAPH
PLAYBILL
PLAYERS
SPORTS
STAR
TICKET
TRADE
VALUE
WRITE

Solution on page 258

Auctions

```
E C I R P C P B G Y T G T L
O L L E S A A R T W O R K A
F I C L E R K I O I L D S N
F S D L G D R C N X E T A D
E T N A W A A G J A Y N L I
R I I C H T N E L I S E E B
E N L C T W W S S J E G V U
U G B L S E U Q I T N A A Y
L E E M L P A I N T I N G G
A S S R U T N E M Y A P B O
V U Y T C I S U L P R U S O
S O L D A B D E Z I E S K D
I H P L A T F O R M V R G S
M O N U M B E R P S M E T I
```

ABSENTEE
AGENT
ANTIQUES
ARTWORK
BARGAIN
BID
BLIND
BUY
CALLER
CARD

CATTLE
CHARITY
CLERK
DEALS
ESTATE
GAVEL
GOING
GOODS
HOUSE
ITEMS

JEWELRY
LAND
LISTING
LIVE
LOT
NUMBER
OFFER
PAINTING
PAYMENT
PLATFORM

PODIUM
PRICE
PROXY
SALE
SEIZED
SELL
SILENT
SOLD
SURPLUS
VALUE

Solution on page 258

At the Dentist

```
B R I D G E D I R O U L F T
J E U Q A L P L S R A L O M
A S E R U T N E D R O N G S
W D E C A Y B G O S G N E R
S A L I V A R G S U I V V I
S I N K T I N I E W O T R A
E R S G N I N A E L C S E H
A N O D H G V H G O A I N C
G L I S B Q C A R O L T A R
D N U L I R F F C S C N M O
G R I K M C A C H E I E E W
B T I T R U N C O N U D L N
F I L L I N G I E S M I L E
E X A M L B S S E S N I R M
```

ACHE	CLEANINGS	FLOSSING	MOLARS
BITING	CROWN	FLUORIDE	NERVE
BRACES	DECAY	GLOVES	ORAL
BRIDGE	DENTIST	GNAW	PLAQUE
BRUSHING	DENTURES	GOLD	RINSE
CALCIUM	DRILL	GRINDING	SALIVA
CANINES	ENAMEL	GUMLINE	SINK
CAVITIES	EXAM	INCISORS	SMILE
CHAIR	FANGS	JAWS	TONGUE
CHEWING	FILLING	LOOSE	

Solution on page 258

Tool

```
T H I P D M E T A L E L I F
P M O W O R K B U F M R U G
E D T E O W B F I S D U D E
G R D R W R E N C H P L S U
W I N C U S K R N L C E G F
O L A S U R E M M A H R A D
B L H A X E N L B T I E W R
W E A N V I L E E N S N X A
A W L D R L R K D S E A T K
L O B T V P C E I R L L A E
E R A B W O R C T R A P S W
V T N L S E K A M T O G K A
E W D A B L A D E B U N R A
L A T H E F P D E V I C E T
```

ANVIL	CUTTER	KNIFE	SCREW
AWL	DEVICE	LATHE	SICKLE
AXE	DRILL	LEVEL	SOCKET
BAND	FILE	MAKE	SPEAR
BELT	GARDEN	METAL	TASK
BLADE	GRINDER	PLANER	TROWEL
BOW	HAMMER	PLIERS	USEFUL
BRUSH	HAND	POWER	WOOD
CHISEL	HOE	RAKE	WORK
CROWBAR	IRON	RULER	WRENCH

Solution on page 259

The International Space Station

```
K R E S E A R C H T R A E G
H O C Y G O L O N H C E T A
E R R E S E N A P A J C F L
G B E C Z T A O L F O P A A
S I W P O S U N O O M R R X
S T F N A S G A P J A O C Y
E X P E R I M E N T S J E T
L A U N C H R O B O U E C I
T N O I T A T S N O R C A L
H Y R O T A R O B A L T P I
G E V I S N E P X E U G S C
I G O V E R N M E N T T V A
E N A S A T E L L I T E S F
W R U S S I A N S T U D Y X
```

ASTRONAUTS	GLOBE	RESEARCH
COOPERATION	GOVERNMENT	RUSSIANS
COSMONAUTS	JAPANESE	SATELLITES
CREW	LABORATORY	SPACECRAFT
EARTH	LAUNCH	STATION
EXPENSIVE	MOON	STUDY
EXPERIMENTS	NASA	SUN
FACILITY	ORBIT	TECHNOLOGY
FLOAT	PROJECT	USA
GALAXY	REPAIR	WEIGHTLESS

Solution on page 259

Bar Scene

```
O R Y I B Q R C R O W D X T
C H X S U O I E H E T B T H
S Y B G P S T S C I L F M M
I T U U H T T G N A A I T
D H L M G O F A L R U X X Z
N M C U O N R J D E E O N D
A G A L D N I S R R S B B Y
B L S T I A E C I G E E O P
E O T S I L N T N L T K O O
E U H A G P D N K A A U T G
R D G N B N S E S S D J H Q
U L I Q U O R V J S O Q G I
S S L F Y G R E N E O N I N
U F E T A L I N E S F V N T
```

ADULTS	DISCO	LATE	PUB
ALE	DRAFT	LAUGHTER	RELAX
BAND	DRINKS	LIGHTS	RHYTHM
BEER	ENERGY	LINES	SINGLES
BOOTH	EVENT	LIQUOR	STOOLS
BOTTLES	FOOD	LOUD	TAB
BOUNCER	FRIENDS	MIXER	TIPS
CLUB	FUN	MUGS	
CROWD	GARNISH	MUSIC	
DANCING	GLASSES	NEON	
DATE	JUKEBOX	NIGHT	

Solution on page 259

68

Newsstand

```
E C N E I N E V N O C S P H
N S I O R O D N E V P O A E
I S E G I Y A L P S I D P A
Z A L R A T H E H E R A L D
A L Y G I R A S C F P B L L
G E D O L A E M I E O B A I
A S N S E L L T R O C U C N
M A A S C R Y S T O I S I E
L H C I D L T H F E F I D G
O C T P I H S F C X S N O A
C R P A S S E R S B Y E I Z
A U D A X E F L L A T S R E
L P C S E M I T E H T S E B
S W E N P O L I T I C S P O
```

ARTICLES	GOSSIP	POLITICS
BOOTH	HEADLINE	PURCHASE
BUSINESS	INFORMATION	SALES
CANDY	LIFESTYLE	SELL
CASH	LOCAL	SERIALS
CIGARETTES	MAGAZINE	SODA
COFFEE	NATIONAL	STALL
CONVENIENCE	NEWS	THE HERALD
DAILY	PAPERS	THE TIMES
DISPLAY	PASSERSBY	VENDOR
GAZEBO	PERIODICAL	

Solution on page 259

Listen to Jazz

```
S O L O A R T I E S H A W T
J N A E R O C K C I H C W O
D O U B L E T I M E T E R M
A S H O W U G R O O V E L M
L K O N D J U M P O B E B Y
L C U K C E B U R B E V A D
A A G N U O Y R E T S E L O
B J E K R A L C Y N N E K R
O T C H O R D T U N E S T S
O L N C I N O M R A H V A E
G I E C O U N T B A S I E Y
I M D B I L L E V A N S B J
E N A M D O O G Y N N E B F
A A C J Z M U R D F F I R W
```

ARTIE SHAW	COOL	LESTER YOUNG
BALLAD	COUNT BASIE	METER
BEAT	DAVE BRUBECK	MILT JACKSON
BEBOP	DOUBLE TIME	RIFF
BENNY GOODMAN	DRUM	SOLO
BILL EVANS	GROOVE	TOMMY DORSEY
BOOGIE	HARMONIC	TUNES
CADENCE	JOHN COLTRANE	
CHICK COREA	JUMP	
CHORD	KENNY CLARKE	

Solution on page 260

Tropical

```
L A G O O N C B T S A N D B
T A N S E O N A C S H A R K
Y D R U C O E J O C E A N W
A I S O F H E P A C S E E R
W M N T C P Q E X K I A E E
A U O I V Y B L N A T T D G
T H R U C T O I T H R O N G
E W K Q L T R I E E L P A A
G A E S I D A R A P A I L E
H V L O M M N T H P N U S M
S E N M A G A I A I H T I R
I S A L T Y N Y K F O O D A
F L O W E R A I V R E T A W
V S Z V A U B Q M R E E F M
```

BANANA	FISH	MAI TAI	SHARK
BEACH	FLOWER	MOSQUITO	SNORKEL
BIKINI	FOOD	OCEAN	STORM
CANOES	FUN	PAPAYA	SUN
CLIMATE	GETAWAY	PARADISE	TANS
COCONUT	HEAT	REEF	TYPHOON
CORAL	HUMID	REGGAE	WARM
DOLPHIN	ISLAND	RETREAT	WATER
DRINKS	LAGOON	SALTY	WAVES
ESCAPE	LOTION	SAND	WEATHER

Solution on page 260

Scholars

```
P D H C R A E S E R U T A M
U O N E P D A C A D E M I A
B C I R U E S L A N R U O J
L T G T N T S C H O O L E D
I O K I I A E N I L T U O T
S R N F V I A W A R D C G I
H A O I E C N S D L E I F N
Y M W C R O S S E F O R P F
R O L A S S M A R T A R D O
A L E T I S Y D U T S U E R
R P D E T A V I T L U C G M
B I G L Y E G E L L O C R E
I D E V O T E D U C A T E D
L I T E R A T E C N R A E L
```

ACADEMIA
ASSOCIATE
AWARD
CERTIFICATE
COLLEGE
CULTIVATED
CULTURED
CURRICULUM
DEGREE
DEVOTED

DIPLOMA
DOCTOR
EDUCATED
FIELDS
INFORMED
JOURNALS
KNOWLEDGE
LEARN
LIBRARY
LITERATE

MATURE
OUTLINE
PEN
PROFESSOR
PUBLISH
RESEARCH
SCHOOLED
SMART
STUDY
UNIVERSITY

Solution on page 260

Hands

```
Y E A I Z J Q W M C H B S Q
Y W N R I N G O N Y T R I D
L H T H D R Y A T N I O P F
D X S H A K E V A W C B A D
F U D B U L Y L C S K I N S
P M N Q C M H C T U L C S H
D G O S H S B R H N E G G O
L L I C D E O T S H E V R L
E J T Y K N I P A T I G I D
H A O N G O A I W O L O P F
C S L I T B R H I O C K M X
U E P W N S E Z V M L L U P
O A M I T T I E V S L I A N
T F O S B R S F Z W S L A P
```

BONES	GENTLE	MITT	SLAP
CATCH	GLOVES	NAILS	SMOOTH
CLAP	GRAB	PAT	SNAP
CLEAN	GRIP	PINKY	SOFT
CLUTCH	HAIRS	POINT	STRONG
DIGIT	HANDS	PULL	THUMB
DIRTY	HELD	PUSH	TICKLE
DRY	HOLD	RING	TOUCH
FIST	JOINTS	SHAKE	WASH
FIVE	LOTION	SKIN	WAVE

Solution on page 260

Explore Outdoors

```
V G N I Z A L B L I A R T A
I G N I P M A C H Y I R N D
E N N T R E K K I N G Y E V
W I I O T P A R K S R O M E
I B A U I A A O I T B S P N
L M R R M T Q M N I O S I T
D I R I M H A U G C O E U U
E L E S U S O E T K T N Q R
R C T M S C F O R E S T E E
N K B U S H W H A C K I N G
E C M S L L I H I P E F U R
S O O A N I M A L S O R F A
S R L O N G D I S T A N C E
C B A C K P A C K I N G X G
```

ADVENTURE	FUN	STICK
ANIMALS	GEAR	SUMMIT
BACKPACKING	HIKING TRAILS	TERRAIN
BOOTS	HILLS	TOURISM
BUSHWHACKING	LONG DISTANCE	TRAILBLAZING
CAMPING	MAP	TREKKING
CROSS COUNTRY	PARKS	VIEW
EQUIPMENT	PATHS	WILDERNESS
FITNESS	RECREATION	
FOREST	ROCK CLIMBING	

Solution on page 261

Cup of Tea

```
C O B G U R T R X M I L K R
Y T R A P I E D R B A G N A
O O E A S C E L E A T E I F
O P W A U R S A A D G D R K
L A N A O U O N I X N U D C
O E S V R M O I N I I E S A
N T A I B P L C F T H N L L
G L T V C E Y I U N T B G B
F S X H E T V D S N O M E L
G N O R T S T E E P O O S P
V T E A R O O M R T S J P I
W H I T E N I M S A J P U S
A L O O C A L M I N G T C D
Y C I P S W E E T N E E R G
```

BAG	DRINK	LOOSE	SPOON
BEVERAGE	FLAVORED	MEDICINAL	STEEP
BLACK	FRUIT	MILK	STIR
BLENDED	GREEN	OOLONG	STRONG
BREW	HOT	PARTY	SUGAR
CALMING	INDIA	RELAXING	SWEET
COOL	INFUSER	SAUCER	TEAPOT
CREAM	JASMINE	SIP	TEAROOM
CRUMPETS	LEAVES	SOOTHING	TISANE
CUPS	LEMON	SPICY	WHITE

Solution on page 261

Trucker

```
T R O P S N A R T E L L A P
T N E M P I H S H I P P E R
R A S N M R B I G R I G E T
E X N E I L O G B O O K C L
C L S D K A X N T K O U A R
E E T Y E A T I G R C N T T
I Z N R U M R N B I I O S E
V C I T U E U B O M S E D R
E A P S S C C R R C F N Y O
R R G U R L K E R I Z G O T
A R N D O E T L N A A I V C
D I I N A U V A O S G N N A
I E K I D F M O E A J E O R
O R L E F L A T B E D A C T
```

AIR BRAKES	DEMURRAGE	MANIFEST	SHIPPER
AXLE	DOCK	OVERSIZE	TANDEM
BIG RIG	ENGINE	PALLET	TERMINAL
BOX TRUCK	FLATBED	RADIO	TIRES
BROKER	FUEL	RECEIVER	TRACTOR
CARRIER	GAS	ROAD	TRANSPORT
CONSIGNOR	INDUSTRY	ROUTE	TRUCKLOAD
CONTAINER	KINGPIN	SEMI	
CONVOY	LOG BOOK	SHIPMENT	

Solution on page 261

On the Radio

```
D I A L K W O H S K L A T K
K C D I S C U S S I O N W B
C O N T E S T S S W E N R P
O M E T A B E D L M N O M O
R M E C I V D A E O A U I P
Y E K C O J C S I D S N C F
R R A P A I I T C E T C R W
T C I Z S T A A V E A E O A
N I Z S R C S A R N Q M P R
U A A E I T W V T U C E H N
O L V D A R I E E I E N O I
C D N T I E N N S U N T N N
A Y I A W N C U L T U R E G
S C O S A Y M B U T T O N S
```

ADVERTISEMENT
ADVICE
AIRWAVES
ANNOUNCEMENT
ANTENNA
BROADCAST
BUTTONS
CLASSICAL
COMMERCIAL

CONTESTS
COUNTRY
CULTURE
DEBATE
DIAL
DISC JOCKEY
DISCUSSION
FREQUENCY
INTERVIEWS

JAZZ
MICROPHONE
MUSIC
NEWS
POP
RAP
ROCK
STATIC
SYNDICATION

TALK SHOW
TUNE
WARNINGS

Solution on page 261

Made of Cotton

```
Y F F U L F S K C O S C H F
R E K N I T T T N A L P I W
O N L Z N F J O F L I G H T
T A F A B R I C W O G D M K
S T P I B S I E R E S R N C
I U Y A R N Y H L O L E A I
H R P D A E R H T D P S P P
L A C G C L J L W U H S J G
L L R W P L I O B E O H D I
I O O V W N O T E R E S E N
M R A B E L I T X E T V N A
G I H N S S S M H B F H I E
R H S H I R T E T I H W M L
N O L W A R M R A F Z R T C
```

BALE	FLUFFY	ORGANIC	THREAD
BOLL	GIN	PANTS	TOWELS
CLEAN	GROW	PICK	WARM
CLOTH	HARVEST	PLANT	WEEVIL
CROP	HISTORY	SEW	WHITE
DENIM	INDIA	SHEETS	WOOL
DRESS	KNIT	SHIRT	YARN
FABRIC	LIGHT	SOCKS	
FARM	LINEN	SOFT	
FIBER	MILL	SOUTH	
FIELD	NATURAL	TEXTILE	

Solution on page 262

Artistic

```
F I N E T P L E A S I N G S
D O G R L C R E A T I V E T
Y R I U V A S K E T C H C Y
N I S T L T N E M G I P U L
A G E X H E Y O S U B T L E
M A D E P I C T I O N E T L
I M T T D J I I U T D T U E
C I T C E L C E T A O F R G
C V I B R A N T H A E M E A
G N I K I R T S I T M B E N
T N I A P P E R S O N A L T
W E I V S Q L A N I G I R O
M O V I N G T Y A L P S I D
S F G N I W O L F R O L O C
```

AESTHETIC	ECLECTIC	PIGMENT
ART	ELEGANT	PLEASING
BEAUTY	EMOTIONAL	SHADE
COLOR	FINE	SKETCH
CREATIVE	FLOWING	STRIKING
CULTURE	INSPIRED	STYLE
DEPICTION	MOVING	SUBTLE
DESIGN	ORIGAMI	TASTEFUL
DISPLAY	ORIGINAL	TEXTURE
DRAMATIC	PAINT	VIBRANT
DYNAMIC	PERSONAL	VIEW

Solution on page 262

Budgets

```
A S T P I E C E R D N E P S
Y E N A K X E D T O L L A L
E L A Y S P C U E I F Z A O
N A R M A E E O N F D T R A
O S G E S N C R U E I E V N
M E A N S S A N S P V C R S
D R M T E E D L A O O E I C
N E A S T S U C Y N N N R T
O S N O N X E R C S I A S T
B E A C U M R A B W I F L I
I R G R O A S W L A C S I F
L V I C C H E C K I N G U O
L E N E C N A L A B F K V R
S I G L A R E D E F N A L P
```

ACCOUNT	CASH	FISCAL	PERSONAL
ALLOT	CHECKING	FUNDS	PLAN
ANALYSIS	COST	GRANT	PROFIT
ASSET	COUPONS	INCOME	RECEIPTS
BALANCE	CREDIT	LOANS	RESERVE
BANK	DEFICIT	LUXURIES	REVENUE
BILLS	EARN	MANAGING	SALES
BOND	EXPENSES	MEANS	SPEND
CAPITAL	FEDERAL	MONEY	
CARRYOVER	FINANCES	PAYMENT	

Solution on page 262

Healthy

```
R X M M P Y V S T U R D Y G
E C I E U R D I T A E E R N
S A W N S S O R T X B L O O
T L S D W I C T A A A I B R
E C A U J Z C L E H L R U T
D I C R O O E R E I A I S S
M U F A E R G G E I N V T R
Y M W N L N O G N X C R A Y
I G O C I M I G I I E S M T
M F R E G M M M I N K R I E
M I K E A F A I G V G L N I
U T O E N O B T N Y R I A D
N P U K C E H C I D L L E W
E B T I U R F L I V E L Y D
```

AGILE	ENDURANCE	MUSCLE	VIGOROUS
BALANCE	ENERGY	PROTEIN	VIRILE
BONE	EXERCISE	RELAXED	VITALITY
BRAIN	FIT	RESTED	VITAMIN
CALCIUM	FRUIT	ROBUST	WALKING
CALM MIND	HARDY	STAMINA	WELL
CHECKUP	IMMUNE	STRENGTH	WORKOUT
DAIRY	JOGGING	STRONG	
DIET	LIVELY	STURDY	
EAT	MINERALS	SWIM	

Solution on page 262

Summertime

```
C H L Y N N U S M I W S E E
E I S X Z W M F D H C A E B
N U N R S A A S P N J I B T
J Y C C E M L L T I E L S A
O I A E I W O N K N D I I N
Y M H L B P O O L I A N R U
P O Y M G R I L L I N G F F
T R I P S N A D F B O G V B
S E L C Y C I B Q H M R G S
K U A X T A E H C U E E A W
R D M E A D O W S M L L R E
A R Y M L A B L C I C A D A
P X V L E V A R T D F X E T
E K I H G R A S S G U B N Y
```

ANTS	FAMILY	HIKE	SAILING
BALMY	FISHING	HOT	SUMMER
BARBECUE	FLOWERS	HUMID	SUNNY
BEACH	FRIENDS	LAZY	SWEATY
BICYCLES	FRISBEE	LEMONADE	SWIM
BLOOMS	FUN	MEADOWS	TAN
BUGS	GARDEN	PARKS	TEA
CAMP	GRASS	PICNIC	TRAVEL
CICADA	GRILLING	POOL	TRIPS
ENJOY	HEAT	RELAX	WALKING

Solution on page 263

Basic Biology

```
E M M O N R A L U L L E C T
N N J R E S E A R C H V E A
E I Z G Y M O T A N A O R X
R E F A N U C L E U S L U O
G T U N V I S S X B I U T N
Y O N I C L G C P F E T C O
D R C S A Y L I E A T I U M
U P T M L A B O R A T O R Y
T D I S S E C T I O N N T D
S N O S I E H U M A N M S U
A D N A U M O L E C U L E S
S C I T E N E G N I W R A D
Y T I D E R E H T W O R G N
T Y N A T O B A C T E R I A
```

ANATOMY	EARTH	LIFE
ANIMALS	ENERGY	MOLECULES
BACTERIA	EVOLUTION	NUCLEUS
BOTANY	EXPERIMENT	ORGANISMS
CELLULAR	FUNCTION	ORIGIN
CHEMISTRY	GENETICS	PROTEIN
CLASS	GROWTH	RESEARCH
DARWIN	HEREDITY	STRUCTURE
DISSECTION	HUMAN	STUDY
DNA	LABORATORY	TAXONOMY

Solution on page 263

Playing Backgammon

```
S L X S T N A I R A V R A B
N U S S N R U T D C R S Y N
W C R E N N I W H I T E G C
A K C A L B E A R O F F E I
P O G A M B L I N G J O T S
A P R O L L A E N G L Y A S
N P G T E D S T E D L B R A
C O U N T E R S R I I E T L
I N G E C P A A M R K A S C
E E D M I C C A U C S V T H
N N I E P C F L E G T E A I
T T C V O U E H H Q H R K P
I E E O N S C I T C A T E S
S F N M S P I P O I N T S D
```

ANCIENT	COUNTERS	OPPONENT	STAKES
BAR	DICE	PAWNS	STONES
BEAR OFF	DRAUGHTS	PIECES	STRATEGY
BEAVER	FAMILY	PIPS	TABLES
BLACK	FUN	POINTS	TACTICS
CASE	GAMBLING	RACCOON	TRIANGLES
CHALLENGE	INDIA	RED	TURNS
CHECKERS	LUCK	ROLL	VARIANTS
CHIPS	MOVEMENT	RULES	WHITE
CLASSIC	OLD	SKILL	WINNER

Solution on page 263

Lunchtime

```
F T S T C B Y M E E T I N G
R U O H R E O T R U G O Y G
F Y I E K H U R R Y L M A S
E P L R T S A F C P L B Z I
S A U M P N O E C I U J Z M
X T T O D O O F C I N C I P
T I O S R E K C A R C P P L
K N M S A N D W I C H T A E
U C P P I T R A K O B A N N
F U I V I E I T L F O S M I
C O E U C C N E I F X O S D
M S R E Q Z K R M E N U O Z
R F S K Q T S L F E P P D Q
B S M R R U S H E D A L A S
```

BAG	FOOD	MENU	SALAD
CHIPS	FORK	MILK	SANDWICH
COFFEE	FRUIT	NAP	SIMPLE
CRACKERS	HAM	PICKLE	SODA
CUPS	HOUR	PICNIC	SOUP
DINE	HURRY	PIZZA	SPOON
DRINKS	JUICE	QUICK	THERMOS
EAT	KNIVES	RECESS	TURKEY
ERRANDS	LUNCHBOX	RELAX	WATER
FAST	MEETING	RUSHED	YOGURT

Solution on page 263

Shows

```
A C T O R S U E E N I T A M
D C O M E D Y Y M A K E U P
N C T E P P U P R R R F D N
U I P I Y C O S T U M E I S
O T A O N A P P L A U S E T
S I T T P G W A D N A T N H
V R R D R C N D A W S I C G
A C I I B U O I A A U V E I
R Q B S Z L C R G O C A V L
I S U P C I D E N N R L E D
E Z T L G V V C U E I B N R
T H E A T E R T P L C S T A
Y N M Y G P R O D U C E R M
I B A L L E T R E C N O C A
```

ACTING	COSTUME	MAGICIAN	THEATER
ACTORS	CRITIC	MAKEUP	TRIBUTE
APPLAUSE	CURTAIN	MATINEE	VARIETY
AUDIENCE	DIRECTOR	OPERA	VEGAS
AWARD	DISPLAY	POPCORN	
BALLET	DRAMA	PRODUCER	
BROADWAY	EVENT	PUPPET	
CIRCUS	FESTIVAL	SINGING	
COMEDY	LIGHTS	SOUND	
CONCERT	LIVE	STAGE	

Solution on page 264

Bodybuilder

```
S T N E M E L P P U S M Y G
W E I G H T L I F T I N G L
F A T T R A C T I V E E A O
S A R A L U C S U M S C Z P
S T S E R I Z N O R I N H H
L S S N D D O W E S C A N Y
L T E E V L Y V Y G R R O S
E E N R T S I H K D E A I I
B R T G P N P U O H X E P Q
B O I Y U H O O B B E P M U
M I F R I I C C R Y R P A E
U D M G N I N N A T D A H T
D S N O I T I T E P M O C O
N O I T I R T U N B C S B A
```

ABS	ENERGY	PHYSICAL
APPEARANCE	EXERCISE	PHYSIQUE
ATTRACTIVE	FITNESS	SPORT
BENCH PRESS	GYM	STEROIDS
BODYBUILDER	HARD	SUPPLEMENTS
CARBOHYDRATES	IRON	TANNING
CHAMPION	MR UNIVERSE	WEIGHTLIFTING
COMPETITIONS	MUSCULAR	WOMEN
CONTESTS	NUTRITION	
DUMBBELLS	OIL	

Solution on page 264

Palm Tree

```
W A R M P L D P O K N U R T
C B M A D A G A S C A R P H
O O G A S C L L T E E S L I
C T N T T I O M R E E A A N
O A I S R P N E O A P R N C
N N P E E O G T P I Z A T L
U I A R S R H T I N L D L I
T C C O E T V O C R S I A M
S I S F D B H A S O Y R T B
R T D N A U A N T F M O S I
O O N I H S W H A I B L A N
U X A A S O A E L L O F O G
G E L R R W I A L A L N C A
H O T G N O I T A C A V B T
```

BOTANIC	GROWN	PLANT	TREES
CALIFORNIA	HAWAII	RAINFOREST	TROPICS
CLIMBING	HEAT	ROUGH	TRUNK
COASTAL	HOT	SAGO	VACATION
COCONUTS	LANDSCAPING	SEA	WARM
CONSERVATION	LONG	SHADE	
DATE PALM	MADAGASCAR	SUBTROPICAL	
DESERTS	OCEAN	SYMBOL	
EXOTIC	PALM OIL	TALL	
FLORIDA	PALMETTO	THIN	

Solution on page 264

Rock Star

```
R N M O N E Y C M B F N V D
S M N G L A M O U R G A O H
H M E V F A N S R O R M I B
O U I T R U O T D A U E C A
W S Y R A T I U G D N I E S
S I T E G L R M D I G F N S
O C Z L C A Z E P E E E E T
N V O R L N Z U D S M R R H
G R O U P I E S T A G E G G
Y W P U L K N I F E C P Y I
D O N O A H V R D N G F J L
P K D M R A D I O U B A N D
S I N G L I A C C L A I M I
N M L X E R I C H J H C S I
```

ACCLAIM	ENERGY	ICON	PUNK
AUDIENCE	FAME	IDOLIZED	RADIO
BAND	FANS	IMAGE	RICH
BASS	FESTIVAL	LIGHTS	ROADIES
BUS	GLAMOUR	MAKEUP	SHOW
CONCERT	GLORY	METAL	SING
COSTUME	GROUPIES	MONEY	SONG
CROWD	GRUNGE	MUSIC	STAGE
DRUM	GUITAR	NAME	TOUR
ELVIS	HAIR	POPULAR	VOICE

Solution on page 264

Family

```
S U P P O R T H U S B A N D
T G S I B L I N G S G E U O
N R P I H S D N E I R F F O
U A I R C S O S H D A I K L
A N H A L S N N L L N W Z B
G D S E O E F I L A D Y D U
E F N L S L H S K C P R A E
N A O C E C E U L I A O U G
E T I U D N C O A G R T G A
A H T N F U E C H O E S H I
L E A T G N I V O L N I T R
O R L G R A N D M O T H E R
G D E D N E T X E I S M R A
Y B R O T H E R H B O N D M
```

AUNTS	GENEALOGY	MARRIAGE
BIOLOGICAL	GRANDCHILDREN	NIECE
BLOOD	GRANDFATHER	NUCLEAR
BOND	GRANDMOTHER	RELATIONSHIPS
BROTHER	GRANDPARENTS	SIBLINGS
CLOSE	HISTORY	SON
COUSINS	HOME	SUPPORT
DAUGHTER	HUSBAND	TREE
EXTENDED	KINSHIP	UNCLES
FRIENDSHIP	LIFE	WIFE
FUN	LOVING	

Solution on page 265

Sleep

```
S B E P G N I M A E R D V O
T E N A R C O L E P S Y M C
E D I S L E E P A P N E A O
K R C H C A S U Q U I E T M
N O I T A N R E B I H W T F
A O D W L I U M M P R X R O
L M E O I G O H C I K E E R
B L M R G H H E A L T H S T
R N I G H T T I M E O D S T
A R R T T M H R E V O C E W
I W D O S A G S T O R Y K B
N C R I B R I N S O M N I A
K L A W P E E L S M E R K B
N Y R A S S E C E N E R G Y
```

ALARM CLOCK	ENERGY	NIGHTTIME
BABY	GROWTH	QUIET
BEDROOM	HEALTH	REM SLEEP
BEDTIME	HIBERNATION	REST
BLANKETS	INSOMNIA	ROBE
BRAIN	LIGHT	SLEEP APNEA
COMFORT	MATTRESS	SLEEPWALK
COVER	MEDICINE	STILL
CRIB	NARCOLEPSY	STORY
DREAMING	NECESSARY	
EIGHT HOURS	NIGHTMARES	

Solution on page 265

Roller Skate

```
C O M P E T I T I O N I P S
N O I T R E X E S L O W H P
R P A N K L A W E D I S E A
E M R S B L A D E S T L L R
N U G L T A E C A P A L M T
T J L E S I C R E X E I E Y
A C I A I D N K Y S R H T H
L I D T S A A G W F C N B I
W S I H S N L P A A E W R N
F U N E A C A E E M R O U L
A M G R H E B B E E E D I I
S T A N C E N V M H N S S N
T O U T D O O R S K W K E E
S T O O B M F R I E N D S R
```

BACKWARDS	DOWNHILL	JUMP	RENTAL
BALANCE	EXERCISE	KNEEPADS	SIDEWALK
BEACH	EXERTION	LACES	SLOW
BLADES	FAST	LEATHER	SPIN
BOOTS	FRIENDS	MOVEMENT	STANCE
BRUISES	FUN	MUSIC	TURN
CHASSIS	GAMES	OUTDOOR	WHEEL
COASTING	GLIDING	PACE	
COMPETITION	HELMET	PARTY	
DANCE	INLINE	RECREATION	

Solution on page 265

Spring Is in the Air

```
K G S D R I B S M R O T S P
T R E A E G R E M E S I R I
S E F F F E S Y S H M G S L
P E I F W A T K T G E A E U
L N L O N I C N M N L R A T
A G H D V U I D O I T D S X
N S A I D C Z M O R G E O T
T L T L A U N F L P N N N H
S C C Y O H P L B S I E I G
A G H N P S T O Q U T W B I
L R I A D W H W Q C S N O L
L A N R E V A E O O E E R D
R S G O R F W R S R N S E U
Y S T U O R P S M C G S I B
```

ACTIVITY	FLOWERS	LIFE	SANDALS
BEES	FROGS	LIGHT	SEASON
BIRDS	GALOSHES	MELT	SHOWERS
BLOOM	GARDEN	NESTING	SPRING
BUD	GRASS	NEWNESS	SPROUT
CROCUS	GREEN	PANSY	STORMS
DAFFODIL	GROWTH	PLANTS	THAW
DUCKS	HATCHING	PUDDLES	TULIP
EMERGE	HYACINTH	RAIN	VERNAL
EQUINOX	IRIS	ROBIN	WARM

Solution on page 265

Made of Silk

```
T H R E A D J A P A N Y S N
E S T C E S N I E T O R P I
X T K P L S M L S C W U I T
T P E I N O A I R O E X D A
U Z A S R F T G E C A U E S
R F P N E T E H B O V L R H
E A B Y T N R T I O I A T T
M B L S T S I F F N N R I O
M R O U A I A H G S G V E O
I I U I P S L E C F S A S M
H C S T H O R A S T E E H S
S A E I O I P A U S C A R F
E B O R E D A R T Q D Y E D
O N O M I K G N O R T S F O
```

ASIA	INSECTS	POPULAR	SOFT
BLOUSE	JAPAN	PROTEIN	SPIDER
CHINESE	KIMONO	QUALITY	STRONG
CLOTHING	LARVAE	ROBE	SUIT
COCOONS	LIGHT	SATIN	TEXTURE
DRESS	LINGERIE	SCARF	THREAD
DYED	LUXURY	SHEETS	TIES
FABRIC	MATERIAL	SHIMMER	TRADE
FASHION	PANTS	SKIRT	WEAVING
FIBERS	PATTERN	SMOOTH	

Solution on page 266

Fast Cars

```
S H T O O M S T E K C I T H
L V O B R U T X R E W O P T
E D A Y F E H C S R O P M O
E E S L M A C H I N E C A R
K E N T U P S C A L E E C Q
J P O S Q A R T S D F L L U
A S T O Q A B R A R E T U E
G M S C L S A L G I R T T K
U O I U E E T T E V R O C C
A T P K G N N M H E A R H I
R O A D W A Y G I R R H E U
P R I C E Y A G I L I T Y Q
B R I D E L B M I N E L O L
S H I F T I N T A K E S L X
```

AGILITY	GAS	PORSCHE	SMOOTH
BRAKES	GEARS	POWER	SPEED
CLUTCH	INTAKE	PRICEY	THRILL
CORVETTE	JAGUAR	QUICK	THROTTLE
COSTLY	MACHINE	RACE	TICKETS
DRIVE	MILES	REV	TORQUE
ENGINE	MOTOR	RIDE	TURBO
EXHAUST	NIMBLE	ROADWAY	UPSCALE
FAST	PISTONS	SHIFT	VALUABLE
FERRARI	POPULAR	SLEEK	

Solution on page 266

Stockbroker

```
T R A H C B W T I H C Z F B
S E L R O O L F G A I N S Q
A P K O D N F U T U R E S B
L T A R S D N U F E C I R P
E S E Y A S R E D I S N I X
C E U C O M P A N Y G N S B
I V L R E U R U L O C E H U
V N A R T T T A O O C U A Y
D I V I D E N D M T A P R I
A N O S O A W E O R L T E E
S D L K N I G R A M L R S L
E E U S L E V E R A G E G D
L X M L S I B T I M I N G Y
L Y E N O M E T O U Q D N G
```

ADVICE	FLOOR	MARGIN	SHARES
ANALYSIS	FUNDS	MARKET	TIMING
BEAR	FUTURES	MONEY	TRADER
BONDS	GAIN	PAYOUT	UPTREND
BUY	GOODWILL	PRICE	VALUE
CALL	INCOME	PUT	VOLUME
CHART	INDEX	QUOTE	YIELD
CHIT	INSIDERS	RISKS	
COMPANY	INVEST	SALE	
DIVIDEND	LEVERAGE	SECTOR	
DOW	LOSS	SELL	

Solution on page 266

Youth

```
F C A M P D J C U L T U R E
S L H H Z O U I S I M L O B
T O E I C O N T D J H A T O
U T L D L H I E I V D U N Y
D H I A G D O G K O D G E S
Y I N L I L R R L D E H M T
I N E L R I I E E I P I F U
N G V O L H S N N S E N E B
G R U W S C S E G C N G A B
N O J A E P S N K O D B R O
U U G N I P O L E V E D L R
O P T C I N N O C E N C E N
Y D R E A M E R S R T O S C
E G A R E D N U F Y B U S Y
```

ADOLESCENT	DEVELOPING	JUVENILE
ALLOWANCE	DISCOVERY	KIDS
BOYS	DREAMERS	LAUGHING
BUSY	ENERGETIC	MENTOR
CAMP	FEARLESS	STUBBORN
CHILDHOOD	FLEDGLING	STUDYING
CHILDREN	FUN	TEENS
CHORES	GIRLS	UNDERAGE
CLOTHING	GROUP	YOUNG
CULTURE	INNOCENCE	
DEPENDENT	JUNIOR	

Solution on page 266

Optical

```
E G A M I P H Y S I C S S B
V S S B T E C H N O L O G Y
R E T C P R O P E R T I E S
E P N O I T C A R F F I D S
N O E U Y T S R O R R I M E
O C M S I R P G L A S E R S
I S U M I C R O S C O P E S
S E R S P E C T R U M D T A
U L T R A V I O L E T E T L
L E S U C O F H V E B A A G
L T N V M P U P I L N I M E
I M I C R O W A V E S S F Y
Z R S E V A W O I D A R E E
S Y A R E F L E C T I O N S
```

DIFFRACTION
EYEGLASSES
FIBER OPTICS
FOCUS
ILLUSION
IMAGE
INSTRUMENTS
LASERS
LENSES
MATTER

MICROSCOPES
MICROWAVES
MIRRORS
NERVE
PHOTOGRAPHY
PHYSICS
PRISM
PROPERTIES
PUPIL
RADIO WAVES

RAYS
REFLECTION
SPECTRUM
TECHNOLOGY
TELESCOPES
ULTRAVIOLET

Solution on page 267

Country Life

```
F B R O O K D F C N R O C A
E S H E E P N I A R G U Q S
N R I T W M D E D A I R Y G
C A U M R O D L R B B L N I
E N T T P E L D T L E W R P
Y C A O A L E S I M O S T V
S H C V K N E S O T U E R F
P R J E Y V S N A K E S A P
O O H R R F A E G A E R C A
R D U A U D H K R T M O T S
C E H L E W H C R O P H O T
D O G L T A N I M A L S R U
B U G S V R D H N L A R U R
T F A M I L Y C O W S B X E
```

ACREAGE	CROPS	HARVEST	RODEO
ANIMALS	DAIRY	HORSES	RURAL
BARN	DIRT	LEMONADE	SHEEP
BLISSFUL	DOG	NATURE	SIMPLE
BROOK	FAMILY	OVERALLS	SLOWER
BUGS	FARM	PASTURE	SNAKES
CAT	FENCE	PIGS	TOWN
CHICKENS	FIELDS	PORCH	TRACTOR
CORN	GARDEN	POULTRY	TREES
COWS	GRAIN	RANCH	WHEAT

Solution on page 267

Occupations

```
N T S I G O L O I B X A S X
S N C R A T H L E T E R S O
U E A E S T R E P O R T E R R
R D S K T S S O G Y U I R O
G I H A R I C I T D D S T S
E S I B O V H B C I U T I S
O E E M N I E C A I D J A E
N R R U A H F M R N S U W F
R P E S U C J X P A K Y A O
O A C I T R K R E L C E H R
T C I C H A S E N A T O R P
C T F I O H I S T O R I A N
O O F A R C I D E M A R A P
D R O N A I R A R B I L D H
```

ACTOR	CARPENTER	OFFICER
ARCHITECT	CASHIER	PARAMEDIC
ARCHIVIST	CHEF	PHYSICIST
ARTIST	CLERK	PRESIDENT
ASTRONAUT	COP	PROFESSOR
ATHLETE	DOCTOR	REPORTER
AUDITOR	HISTORIAN	SENATOR
AUTHOR	JUDGE	SURGEON
BAKER	LIBRARIAN	WAITRESS
BANKER	MAID	
BIOLOGIST	MUSICIAN	

Solution on page 267

Hardware Store

```
A C I M H E B C H A I N N S
L C L C C L F P L I E R S C
A S E I K L U A C E N L N R
T L V P L H S M O A V G F E
N E O F I E P B E U E E W
E W H C I P S K L E P G L S
R O S C K L A I M P R O V E
Y D V E T L T I H I E W R A
R E P I L A C E N C M I S L
L N K I L W R D R T M R I A
R F R A I Y E W A S A E A N
P D W G A R D E N E H C X T
T N T U N D J R H C N E R W
B O L T O O L S W O O D L T
```

ACE	GARDEN	NUT	SHOVEL
BOLT	GRINDER	PAINT	TILE
CALIPER	HAMMER	PIPE	TOOLS
CAULK	HINGES	PLIERS	VICE
CHAIN	IMPROVE	RATCHET	WIRE
CHISEL	KEY	RENTAL	WOOD
DOWELS	LAWN	ROPE	WRENCH
DRILL	LEVEL	SAW	
DRYWALL	LOCK	SCREWS	
FILTERS	LUMBER	SEALANT	
FUSES	NAIL	SHEARS	

Solution on page 267

Memorial Day

```
S E R V I C E G A R U O C S
R O L A V O L U N T E E R R
H O L I D A Y S N O L N F E
H O N O R M L O P E N L L W
M A Y E I G I D B A O I A O
R Q N H C T M R R B T S G L
O U D G A I A P A Y G T I F
F Y E N C T F R V T N E N H
I T C I E A B I E U I D F I
N R E N J E D D R D L O A S
U E A R C B V E Y C R W N T
S B S U W S E L T T A B T O
L I E O F F I C E R S S R R
O L D M W M I L I T A R Y Y
```

ADMIRATION	FAMILY	MOURNING
ARLINGTON	FLAG	NATION
BARBECUE	FLOWERS	OFFICERS
BATTLES	FUNERAL	PRIDE
BRAVERY	HISTORY	SACRIFICE
CADET	HOLIDAY	SERVICE
CELEBRATE	HONOR	TAPS
COURAGE	INFANTRY	UNIFORM
DECEASED	LIBERTY	VALOR
DUTY	MAY	VOLUNTEER
ENLISTED	MILITARY	WAR

Solution on page 268

Waiter

```
I X E F Y C E N H Y A R T O
M R S G T K H W O R K I W P
I E L E N D A E R E N N I D
O F A U T I P H C N U R B I
W I I J T R N N Y K C J N X
Y L C R M L A I R I O N G D
A L E H S L U E D B F R C S
I S P C A R V N Y A F E Y R
S K S B F R E V I L E D O D
B N M W E H M N S F E R O A
L I E S C T W I N E O O B D
P R N N A P K I N A F R G M
H D U B Z B O G W G M V M Z
T L S M I L E X U S D N N K
```

BALANCE	JOB	TEA
BREAD	LUNCH	TIP
BRUNCH	MANNERS	TRAY
CHARMING	MENUS	UNIFORM
CHECK	NAPKIN	WAITRESS
COFFEE	ORDER	WINE
DELIVER	REFILLS	WORK
DINING	SERVER	
DINNER	SMILE	
DRINKS	SPECIALS	
FOOD	TAB	

Solution on page 268

Cities Around the World

```
W I K C A I R O Y E N D Y S
O T O R O N T O G A C I H C
C R K G A N O L E C R A B L
S A G N M I A M I T N A E A
O F N I S S O P S G G V D L
M F A J T R E E H H A U I M
T I B I E N P A D R B M O N
B C R E R A I A T L A N T A
O Y U B D P D L I T T L T I
S T R U A V O N R R L H A R
T I B J M N N R E E E E W O
O N A J D I B A T N B C A B
N L U O E S L E S S U R B I
V E N I C E M A D R I D H G
```

ABIDJAN	BERLIN	MADRID	SEOUL
AIRPORTS	BOSTON	MIAMI	SHANGHAI
AMSTERDAM	BRUSSELS	MONTREAL	SYDNEY
ATHENS	BUDAPEST	MOSCOW	TORONTO
ATLANTA	CAIRO	NAIROBI	TRAFFIC
BAGHDAD	CHICAGO	OTTAWA	TRAVEL
BANGKOK	DUBLIN	RIO	URBAN
BARCELONA	LIMA	ROME	VENICE
BEIJING	LONDON	SEATTLE	

Solution on page 268

Ads Everywhere

```
F S M S N A G O L S O B O Y
L E C E A S D A B P N A G E
Y R O M S T N I U A L N O N
E U M I E S T G S M I N L O
R T P F D D A E I D N E A M
S C A M P A I G N S E R U P
R I N T E C R A E T H S D R
O P Y N N X R C S S I Y I O
S A L E S B O T S O C O E D
N M G T E U N E V E R A N U
O A Q N P G N I H T O L C C
P I Y O P R I N T E R N E T
S L N C A R S P O S T E R S
J S E L L I N G J I N G L E
```

ADS	CLOTHING	MAIL	PRODUCTS
AGENCIES	COMPANY	MEDIA	RADIO
ATTENTION	CONTENT	MESSAGES	REVENUE
AUDIENCE	COST	MONEY	SALES
BANNERS	COUPONS	ONLINE	SELLING
BRANDING	FLYERS	PENS	SIGNS
BUSINESS	INTERNET	PICTURES	SLOGANS
CAMPAIGNS	JINGLE	POSTERS	SPAM
CARS	LOGO	PRINT	SPONSOR

Solution on page 268

Landscaping

```
T F E E G G O X S S P E U H
K R O C K S W C N H O N O C
M U I Y H A E K D O T U G L
X T Q M T N R V E V S R R U
E D G E I T M Q O E K P A M
H F R C A B E K A L R M S L
T M H M M C A R I N G C S A
A O V I S U A L P E X F B W
P W O S O R C H A R D L U N
J E D T D E S I G N W O R G
R E P O N D R A Y K C W H H
B D T N A L P E B B L E S I
W S E E R T M Y N E D R A G
A V M P C B A G S E H S U B
```

BAGS	GARDEN	PATH	SHOVEL
BALANCE	GLOVES	PEBBLES	SHRUBS
BEDS	GRASS	PLANT	STONE
BUSHES	GROWN	POND	TREES
CARING	HOUSE	POTS	TRIM
CHOP	LAKE	PRETTY	TURF
CREEK	LAWN	PRUNE	VISUAL
DESIGN	MOW	RAKE	WATER
EDGE	MULCH	ROCKS	WEED
FLOWERS	ORCHARD	SCENIC	YARD

Solution on page 269

Buying a House

```
D E Q U I T Y M O V I N G A
A P P R A I S A L O F F E R
M A R K E T S C L O S I N G
E M O H I L I S T I N G S R
N A O L L E G A G T R O M E
I N S U R A N C E M E N P Y
T E G D U B V R L P D O R U
I C T I T L E O U R N I O B
E O A P C S C R R O E T C R
S B R R T A C B T P L C U O
E T N Q T H A A T E P U R K
X A W I A N R A S R X A E E
A I O S K Y O R O T L A E R
T N E M Y A P C C Y D E E D
```

AMENITIES	COST	MARKET	PURCHASE
APPRAISAL	DEED	MORTGAGE	REALTOR
APPROVAL	EQUITY	MOVING	SIGN
AUCTION	HOME	NOTARY	TAXES
BANK	INSURANCE	OBTAIN	TITLE
BROKER	INTEREST	OFFER	
BUDGET	LENDER	OWN	
BUYER	LISTINGS	PAYMENT	
CLOSING	LOAN	PROCURE	
CONTRACT	LOCATION	PROPERTY	

Solution on page 269

Jump on a Trampoline

```
T S I W T R A I N I N G B S
E E R F A L L I N G P E U D
D L E E T S U J L A L C G A
I S A F C T U A D A R B N N
V S G N I R P S S I T E I G
I P R T Y E E T C R D J C E
N K A E G T I A I E E U N R
G D V N N C T B T S L M U O
C N I Y I H R O S I I P O U
I U T T L R A R A C O I B S
R O Y E B O P C N R C N R J
B B T F M U E A M E H G I H
A E O A U N Z U Y X P L A Y
F R T S T D E Z G E M A R F
```

ACROBATS	FABRIC	PADS	STRETCH
AIR	FALLING	PLAY	TRAINING
ATHLETE	FRAME	REBOUND	TRAPEZE
BOUNCING	FREE	RECREATION	TUMBLING
CIRCUS	GRAVITY	ROUND	TWIST
COILED	GYMNASTICS	SAFETY NET	
DANGEROUS	HIGH	SIT	
DIVING	INJURY	SOMERSAULT	
ELASTICITY	JUMPING	SPRINGS	
EXERCISE	MAT	STEEL	

Solution on page 269

Accountant

```
S C O M P U T E C N A L A B
M B L K C S N M U L O C U T
R J U A O Y I E L N C R D I
O S S D T O C I A O H E I F
F H T I G I B H U I E D T O
X I U E O E P N R T C I J R
R Q G V S E T A C I K T N P
E Q N U S S P X C D H A A A
G I I W R N A T A D T Y O Y
D P A Y M E N T I A A U L R
E L I F Z P S R E B M U N O
L O S S E X A T L F E E S L
S N R U T E R E C O R D S L
K G R E V E N U E M O C N I
```

ACCOUNTS	CASH	FIGURES	NUMBERS
ACCRUAL	CHECK	FILE	PAYABLE
ADDITION	COLUMNS	FORMS	PAYMENT
ASSETS	COMPUTE	INCOME	PAYROLL
AUDIT	CREDIT	INVOICE	PROFIT
BALANCE	DATA	LAWS	RECORDS
BILL	DEBIT	LEDGER	RETURNS
BOOK	EQUITY	LOAN	REVENUE
BUDGET	EXPENSE	LOSS	TAXES
CAPITAL	FEES	MATH	

Solution on page 269

Dear Diary

```
A T T N U O C C A N C W I H
D H N O E L C I N O R H C I
N O O N V N Q E N I P L O D
E U I P E O P F T T R E V E
G G T U N I E E W C O T E T
A H O B T S E C R E T T R A
S T M L S S G N I L E E F V
M S E I S A T N A F C R R I
A D O C Y P D A T E T S E R
E N Z R D E H S I R E H C P
R E A U G N I W A R D D O S
D I N S I G H T B O O K R A
D R R H J O U R N A L P D L
Z F A M I L Y R T E O P V C
```

ACCOUNT	DATE	FRIENDS	PLAN
AGENDA	DIARY	HIDE	POETRY
BOOK	DRAWING	INSIGHT	PRIVATE
CHERISHED	DREAMS	JOURNAL	PROTECTED
CHRONICLE	EMOTION	LETTERS	RECORD
CLASP	EVENTS	LOG	REFLECTION
CONFESSION	FAMILY	NONPUBLIC	SECRET
COVER	FANTASIES	PASSION	THOUGHTS
CRUSH	FEELINGS	PEN	WRITE

Solution on page 270

Statistical Analysis

```
T S K E S D E V I A T I O N
N N D Y Q H X M E D I A N S
E O O T P O P U L A T I O N
M I I I A S E A P P M P I O
E T S T T S R K R A P R S I
R C E N A A I Q T G V O S T
U I R A D L M H H K A B E A
S D U U T C E R E K R A R U
A E G Q R M N R O N I B G Q
E R I F A C T S R F A I E E
M P F T H H S X Y O N L R G
N O I T C E L L O C C I R N
A C T U A R I A L B E T O A
S E G A T N E C R E P Y R R
```

ACTUARIAL	EXPERIMENTS	PERCENTAGES
CHART	FACTS	POPULATION
CLASS	FIGURES	PREDICTIONS
COLLECTION	GRAPHS	PROBABILITY
CORRELATION	INFORMATION	QUANTITY
DATA	MATHEMATICS	RANGE
DEVIATION	MEASUREMENT	REGRESSION
EQUATIONS	MEDIAN	THEORY
ERROR	MODE	VARIANCE

Solution on page 270

Invitation

```
R A X H O L I D A Y H X Q E
E T A V I R P L L S T A M P
Q T P M O R P L I T N O F D
U E A F E G A R U O C N E A
E N P P L I U G O L F L E I
S D E O D O Y S E P I P N Q
T A R R L R C W S V O V G D
P N O F M E N A E O I S R E
E C D H N S V R T T B R A C
C E M I T P I N E I N M V L
C A L L N O A T E W O E E I
A N D E T N I R P U O N V N
O C A R D S E E T A D H H E
G N I D D E W R Z Y B K S A
```

ACCEPT	DINNER	INVITE	RESPONSE
ASK	EMBOSS	LOCATION	RSVP
ATTENDANCE	ENCOURAGE	ONLINE	SHOWER
BAPTISM	ENGRAVE	PAPER	STAMP
CALL	ENVELOPE	PARTY	TIME
CARD	EVENT	PRINTED	WEDDING
CORDIALLY	FLOURISH	PRIVATE	WELCOME
DATE	FOIL	PROMPT	
DECLINE	FONT	PROPOSAL	
DELIVER	HOLIDAY	REQUEST	

Solution on page 270

Field Trip

```
C L Y M U S E U M V I S I T
L L E S S O N E R D L I H C
A S C V A M O N U M E N T T
S N Z A A D E O P E R A E H
S V E O P R V R U O T L E E
E P P T O I T E K N U J Q A
E R U L S V T P N D N S S T
C F P O A I I A E T C P O E
N X S U R N L H L F U I U R
E T T T S G C C B U L R V H
I I U I H S J A U N T T E C
C M D N O E D I S T U O N N
S E Y G W H I S T O R Y I U
T I C K E T E A C H E R R L
```

ADVENTURE	GROUPS	OPERA	THEATER
BUS	HISTORY	OUTING	TICKET
CAPITAL	INSIDE	OUTSIDE	TIME
CHAPERONE	JAUNT	PLAN	TOUR
CHILDREN	JUNKET	SCHEDULE	TRAVEL
CLASS	LESSON	SCIENCE	TRIPS
CULTURE	LISTEN	SHOW	VISIT
DRIVING	LUNCH	SOUVENIR	ZOO
EXPLORE	MONUMENT	STUDY	
FUN	MUSEUM	TEACHER	

Solution on page 270

Corporate Culture

```
S X H V H M O O R L I A M V
E N A M R I A H C I L B U P
G F H U T N E D I S E R P J
A U L C S E C R E T A R Y M
S E I T R O I V A H E B T D
S S I D T A L A M R O F I R
E E C N E R E F N O C V U I
M L L M L L Y S U B I H S T
A C I I E E I S E S S T Y U
N I E S P L G N I R A H S A
N B N S H Y J O E S K I L L
E U T I O T N A T S I S S A
R C S O N S T R U C T U R E
S B E N E F I T S Y L A N A
```

ANALYST	FORMAL	RITUAL
ASSISTANT	GUIDELINES	RULES
BEHAVIOR	HIERARCHY	SECRETARY
BENEFITS	MAIL ROOM	SHARING
BUSY	MANNERS	SKILL
CHAIRMAN	MESSAGES	STRUCTURE
CLIENTS	MISSION	STYLE
CONFERENCE	PRESIDENT	SUIT
CUBICLES	PUBLIC	TELEPHONE
DIVISIONS	RESEARCH	TIE

Solution on page 271

Weather Forecast

```
M R O T S E E R G E D T P S
F L T E E L S N D L O C U Z
L H U M I D I T Y R O I H D
U O Z P K H A G N L S O I R
R V W E C L D A H L T R C I
R E W R M F D R E T E Y F Z
I R O A N O E C A C N T R Z
E C N T I G W Q T Z C I O L
S A S E A D P I W H Z V N E
C S F R R X O H A I L I T G
L T E O D N I W V G H T L K
E V C C H A N C E H I C E B
A E F Y R E T E M O R A B M
R D R O U G H T H U N D E R
```

ACTIVITY	DEGREES	HIGH	SLEET
ALMANAC	DEW POINT	HOT	SNOW
AVERAGE	DIRECTION	HUMIDITY	STORM
BAROMETER	DRIZZLE	ICE	TEMPERATE
BLIZZARD	DROUGHT	LIGHTNING	THUNDER
CELSIUS	FLURRIES	LOW	TORNADO
CHANCE	FOG	OVERCAST	WIND
CLEAR	FRONT	RAIN	
COLD	HAIL	RECORD	
COOL	HEAT WAVE	SCORCHING	

Solution on page 271

Gardener

```
S B U S H E S C E N E R Y C
E H E R B S I E E H O E R M
E B H K D N D N C N D T E U
D U S R A I U S U N N A L L
S L I G G R T S T R E W E C
A B R C P L N S T I T F C H
V O U L A I N N E I B U A G
F L O W E R S R L V W B R C
R A N M G A R D E N R E A E
U U T S O P M O C M E A E R
I N G L O V E S T N M U H D
T N S W O R Y R E S R U N B
H A E P L A N T S Q U A S H
F E D A P S L O O T O I L O
```

ANNUAL	FLOWERS	NOURISH	SEEDS
BIENNIAL	FRUIT	NURSERY	SOD
BIRDS	GARDEN	NURTURE	SPADE
BULB	GLOVES	ORGANIC	SQUASH
BUSHES	GREEN	PLANTS	SUMMER
CARROTS	HARVEST	PRUNE	TEND
CELERY	HERBS	RABBITS	TOIL
COMPOST	HOE	RAKE	TOOLS
DIG	LETTUCE	ROWS	WATER
FENCE	MULCH	SCENERY	WEED

Solution on page 271

Collecting Coins

```
D  L  G  G  N  I  D  A  R  T  C  E  N  T
Y  E  N  O  M  N  C  S  Y  E  D  U  V  C
T  N  I  M  Y  V  E  O  N  I  V  P  A  O
C  Q  D  D  D  E  T  E  U  E  T  L  R  I
E  U  A  O  E  S  A  G  L  N  K  F  I  N
J  A  R  I  A  T  D  R  E  G  T  O  E  S
B  R  G  R  L  M  A  I  O  P  A  R  T  K
U  T  P  E  E  E  C  L  R  E  E  E  Y  O
S  E  E  P  R  N  A  E  U  J  R  I  B  O
M  R  N  P  A  T  C  Q  D  C  A  G  B  B
U  T  N  O  A  I  I  Y  L  J  R  N  O  U
B  Y  I  C  O  T  Y  R  O  T  S  I  H  T
L  P  E  U  N  O  I  T  I  D  N  O  C  K
A  E  S  A  D  R  A  O  H  M  E  T  A  L
```

ALBUMS	COUNTRY	HOBBY	RARE
ANCIENT	CURRENCY	INVESTMENT	SILVER
ANTIQUE	DATE	METAL	SUBJECT
BOOKS	DEALER	MINT	TOKENS
CATALOG	EAGLE	MONEY	TRADING
CENT	FOREIGN	OLD	TYPE
CIRCULATED	GRADING	PENNIES	VARIETY
COINS	GUIDE	PERIOD	YEAR
CONDITION	HISTORY	PRECIOUS	
COPPER	HOARD	QUARTER	

Solution on page 271

Kitchen Tools

```
F G H J B S T R A I N E R C
R R R A B L H R R E L D A L
Y E E I L U E N E V O N J E
I P K X L M R N Y L O S M A
N P M A I L M N D P I T I V
G O A T M M O U E E X O C E
P H S R R E M N C R R P R R
A C H E E S E C L O T H O B
N T E D P R T F K S I H W O
E O R N P P E E F I N K A W
L N M A E U R S P O O N V L
A G L L P C O R K S C R E W
C S F O R K E R U S A E M C
S A U C E P A N I T E I P H
```

BLENDER	CUP	PEPPER MILL
BOWL	FORK	PIE TIN
BROILER	FRYING PAN	POTS
BURNER	GRILL	SAUCEPAN
CAN OPENER	KNIFE	SCALE
CHEESECLOTH	LADLE	SPOON
CHOPPER	MASHER	STRAINER
CLEAVER	MEASURE	THERMOMETER
COFFEEMAKER	MICROWAVE	TIMER
COLANDER	MIXER	TONGS
CORKSCREW	OVEN	WHISK

Solution on page 272

Storage

```
H O L D I N G S T A S H K D
K E E P S A K E S E N C N E
C S O R T I N G H G R E U H
O U S E U Q I T N A A L J S
L O A T S T O W T K B L P G
D H S T O L I E T C E A A A
A E E U C V S N A A C R C R
P R A L S P E S R P I E K A
Y A S C B M I R C U F D I G
B W O T E O L E H D F I N E
B I N S W V P W I E O V G C
U S A U B I P A V Z A I J A
C B L D O N U R E H I D E P
A T T I C G S D S E X O B S
```

ANTIQUES   CRATE   MOVING   STOW
ARCHIVES   CUBBY   OFFICE   SUPPLIES
ATTIC   DIVIDER   OVERHEAD   WAREHOUSE
BARN   DRAWERS   PACKAGE
BASEMENT   DUST   PACKING
BINS   FURNITURE   PADLOCK
BOXES   GARAGE   SEASONAL
CELLAR   HIDE   SHED
CLOTHES   HOLDING   SORTING
CLUTTER   JUNK   SPACE
COBWEBS   KEEPSAKES   STASH

Solution on page 272

Smart Words

```
K U S D E T F I G Y N N A C
N N S C P R O D I G Y P R E
O D O C H E D U C A T E D S
W E Y W H O R D W E R H S I
I R N M L O O C R A F T Y W
N S I N T E L L E C T U A L
G T A S E N D A E P A W C E
A A R U A E A G R D T H L T
S N B I M G K I E L K I E A
T D E N R A E L L A Y Z V R
U I C E R E B R A L B H E E
T N E G I L L E T N I L R T
E G G H E A D E P T D R E I
W Y E X P E R T H G I R B L
```

ADEPT	EGGHEAD	PERCEPTIVE
APT	EXPERT	PRODIGY
ASTUTE	GENIUS	SAGE
BRAINY	GIFTED	SCHOLARLY
BRIGHT	INTELLECTUAL	SCHOOLED
BRILLIANT	INTELLIGENT	SHREWD
CANNY	KEEN	UNDERSTANDING
CEREBRAL	KNOWING	WHIZ
CLEVER	KNOWLEDGEABLE	WISE
CRAFTY	LEARNED	
EDUCATED	LITERATE	

Solution on page 272

Mother's Day

```
H T M R A W B L U N C H H L
S L E E P O S G U H R E O D
K J J S U R P R I S E V N R
N E W Q E R E L A X E D O A
A W U W S E D U T I T A R G
H E O D B R E A K F A S T E
T L C I E S C H E R I S H R
F R A N U M O M B R U N C H
I Y N N R E R U T R U N O D
G C D E H E A R T F E L T R
M A Y R E S T E E M I S P A
Y K S E S S I K R D R A C W
C E C H O C O L A T E S T E
V A L U E D N Y L R A E Y R
```

BOUQUET	ESTEEM	LUNCH	SURPRISE
BREAKFAST	FLOWERS	MAY	THANKS
BRUNCH	GIFT	MOM	VALUED
CAKE	GRATITUDE	NURTURER	WARMTH
CANDY	HEARTFELT	REGARD	YEARLY
CARD	HOLIDAY	RELAXED	
CHERISH	HONOR	REST	
CHILDREN	HUGS	REWARD	
CHOCOLATES	JEWELRY	SLEEP	
DECORATION	KISSES	SPA	
DINNER	LOVE	SUNDAY	

Solution on page 272

Hooray for Hollywood

```
A C A D E M Y A W A R D S N
E G P I R T S T E S N U S G
M S O S U H C I R K S P O I
A T P T T H I S T O R I C S
F E U R C C N B C D O S E E
F L L I I I E U E A T S A L
O E A C P T M L L K C O N E
K V R T N Y A C E T A G E G
L I D O O H R O B H G I E N
A S L L I H Y L R E V E B A
W I T S T A R S I A C A R S
E O P E O P L E T T R Z T O
S N F A M O U S Y R X T X L
T E S O I D U T S E I V O M
```

ACADEMY AWARDS
ACTORS
ART
BEVERLY HILLS
CARS
CELEBRITY
CINEMA
CITY
CLUBS
DISTRICT

FAMOUS
GOSSIP
HISTORIC
KODAK THEATRE
LOS ANGELES
MOTION PICTURE
MOVIE STUDIOS
NEIGHBORHOOD
OCEAN
PEOPLE

POPULAR
RICH
SIGN
STARS
SUNSET STRIP
TELEVISION
WALK OF FAME
WEST

Solution on page 273

Bears

```
Y Z A B B I G N I R A M T Q
D B L A C K E R U S S A E L
D S A W T E C F I S H M E H
E R O V I N R A C Z C M T T
T J K G H L T O T L Z A H R
L A N R U I D Y V T J L V E
O N A B C E E S Y I A G Y E
B O E K R K R L E E N O I G
R M B D O O S U R I N M R F
P L V M D D W W T R C O O O
U A S L A M I N A A W E H R
B S N Z Z B U A P L N F P E
W O O D S H L A K O C U B S
M O M E A T S W A P O O H T
```

ANIMAL	CUB	KOALA	ROAR
ASIATIC	DEN	KODIAK	SALMON
ATTACK	DIURNAL	MAMMAL	SMOKEY
BAMBOO	FISH	MEAT	SPECIES
BIG	FOREST	NATURE	TEDDY
BLACK	FUR	OMNIVORE	TEETH
BROWN	GRIZZLY	PANDA	TREE
CARNIVORE	GROWL	PAWS	WILD
CAVE	HONEY	POLAR	WOODS
CLAWS	HUNTING	POOH	ZOO

Solution on page 273

Paying the Bills

```
L U D S T N E M Y A P A I D
I E T E I N T E R E S T A X
A G H I L G C T N U O C C A
M R T R L I N H R E T A W R
E A E E C I N A E O L D T E
C H N C L O T Q T C P U F C
N C I O W E L I U U K E A E
A T L R F C P L E E R S R I
N N D G D E A H E S N E D P
I U A R L T E S O C W T R T
F O E G O O D S H N T B E D
B M D R A C K N A B E I V Q
B A L A N C E G A G T R O M
R E T S I G E R E G D E L N
```

ACCOUNT	DEADLINE	LEDGER	RECEIPT
AMOUNT	DEBT	LOAN	RECORD
BALANCE	DELINQUENT	MAIL	REGISTER
BANK CARD	DUE	MORTGAGE	REPORT
CALCULATOR	FEES	OVERDRAFT	SIGNATURE
CASH	FINANCE	OWE	TAX
CHARGE	GOODS	PAID	TELEPHONE
CHECKS	GROCERIES	PAYMENTS	UTILITIES
COLLECTION	INTEREST	RATE	WATER

Solution on page 273

Boeing Jumbo Jet

```
S E N G I N E S T H G I L F
W C T S A F A I R C R A F T
I O A I R P O R T E W E R C
D N F F O E K A T N C S P H
E O I S B I G H H N U J C T
B M K B N H G N A P U A R Y
O Y A L A I C R E M M O C A
D T I T E C F R B S P G O I
Y I R R S R S O T S S R C R
T R F B I O J O N H R A K P
E U O A N E L A R G E C P L
F C R I T I R E N I L R I A
A E C S P T E V E R E T T N
S S E N I S U B O E I N G E
```

AIR FORCE	CABIN	FLIGHTS	SECURITY
AIR FRANCE	CARGO	FREIGHTER	SKY
AIRCRAFT	COCKPIT	JETS	SUPERSONIC
AIRLINER	COMMERCIAL	JUMBO JET	TAKEOFF
AIRPLANE	CREW	LARGE	TRANSPORT
AIRPORT	ECONOMY	MACH	WIDE BODY
BIG	ENGINES	PASSENGERS	
BOEING	EVERETT	PILOTS	
BUSINESS	FAST	SAFETY	

Solution on page 273

Painter

```
S L L A W E N K X E T A L L
E I A S P R A Y A A C I J E
B O R A P T C B L R A N P S
C P T B X O S E E P A R N A
C A I A A T N A H C I I R E
O L S L R T T G R M A O O S
L E T A E O A Y E T L T T A
O T C N R K L R S L N A B B
R T A C E I O E E W R O U H
I E G E C M I R T P N C C S
M E D I U M G R T S M T K U
U F U D E L L I K S E E E R
S E T T A M A T P K A A T B
E I S S O L G S S M E L L S
```

ABSTRACT	CONTRAST	PAIL	SPRAY
ACRYLIC	CREATOR	PALETTE	STAINS
ARTIST	EASEL	PIGMENT	STIRRER
BALANCE	GLOSS	PRIMER	STROKE
BASE	LADDER	ROLLER	TALENT
BRUSH	LATEX	SEAL	TAPE
BUCKET	MATTE	SKETCH	TARP
CAN	MEDIUM	SKILLED	TEMPERA
COAT	MUSE	SMELLS	TRIM
COLOR	OIL	SPONGE	WALLS

Solution on page 274

Public Transit

```
C M E T R O L L E Y B O A T
P M S N R L I A R T H G I L
P A C E S A M T R A K R E T
O A E O N C F O G R E E N I
L I S H M I H F N V R E A M
L R Y S C M L E I O I T L E
U C A T E O U R D C R S P T
T R W E S N D T I U T A R A
I A L K Y O G F E A L A I B
O F I C A C F E T R I E A L
N T A I W E D I R N S X S E
U B R T B P O T S S U B A Q
N A B R U N S E I T I C O T
F A R E S E I R R E F A S T
```

AIRCRAFT	DRIVER	PASSENGERS	TIMETABLE
AIRLINES	ECONOMICAL	POLLUTION	TRAFFIC
AIRPLANE	EFFICIENT	RAILWAY	TRAINS
AMTRAK	FARES	RIDE	TROLLEY
BOAT	FAST	SAFE	URBAN
BUS STOP	FERRIES	SCHEDULES	
CAB	GREEN	STATIONS	
CHEAP	LIGHT RAIL	SUBWAYS	
CITIES	METRO	TAXI	
COMMUTERS	MONORAIL	TICKETS	

Solution on page 274

Appearances

```
T N A G E L E D Y N I H S B
R U V D C P C D E S I O P E
E G E I O E L L U D D E G X
L L R S L R M E E K W M G O
A Y A T O L A O A A L O K T
T H G I R B U B G S R S R I
S T E N F S P F L G I D A C
S L X C U T E L E E B N D L
E I C T L Z C O A C D A G O
L F I Y D D U M M U A H R U
T A T W V S L G I I S R C D
O I E P L A I N N E S U G Y
P R D S T R A N G E T T N G
S U O I C E R P R E T T Y U
```

ADORABLE	DISTINCT	GRACEFUL	PRETTY
ALERT	DRAB	HANDSOME	SHINY
AVERAGE	DULL	HIDEOUS	SPOTLESS
BRIGHT	ELEGANT	MISTY	STRANGE
CLEAR	EXCITED	MUDDY	UGLY
CLOUDY	EXOTIC	PECULIAR	UNUSUAL
COLORFUL	FAIR	PLAIN	
CROWDED	FILTHY	PLEASING	
CUTE	GLEAMING	POISED	
DARK	GORGEOUS	PRECIOUS	

Solution on page 274

Fun Activities

```
C Y D W G M O V I E S E W V
A L R T H E A T E R C B G C
M I C I R C U S Z O O O S G
P M G U A B D A N C E W E A
I A N T S K I C K B A L L M
N F I G A E E K C M H I Z E
G O G N R R O T E I G N Z S
N G N I T T I N K R N G U T
I B I H E I I I I Y I C P R
T E M S U C N A X M R D I O
I A M I Q G F G F A O E E P
R C I F O O T B A L L D A S
W H W F R I E N D S O E U D
M U S I C R A F T S C G R O
```

ART	CROQUET	HIKING	RUN
BEACH	DANCE	KICKBALL	SEW
BIKE RIDE	DOMINOES	KNITTING	SPORTS
BOWLING	FAIR	MOVIES	SWIMMING
CAMPING	FAMILY	MUSIC	THEATER
CINEMA	FISHING	PAINTING	VACATION
CIRCUS	FOOTBALL	PICNIC	WRITING
COLORING	FRIENDS	PUZZLES	ZOO
CONCERT	GAMES	READ	
CRAFTS	GOLF	RELAX	

Solution on page 274

Plumber

```
T C L O G A S D V A L V E N
R A S E W A G E R P X I F R
T U N I F O R M L A T E M I
O L S K R U I U E E I E Y A
O K Z T S E N N L R G N V H
L V T S V G P I S A P D S B
P E E T E S O A K T L E U U
I R K R X T E C I O A L P T
P E C A F K O R K R S L P U
E W U D N L A T V N T I L F
S O B E B S O E R I I K Y X
S H R E H S A W L U C S Q K
E S I P H O N F A U C E T P
M R E T A W R E N C H K R H
```

AERATOR	INSTALL	RUST	TOILET
BLOCKAGE	LEAK	SERVICE	TOOL
BUCKET	MESS	SEWAGE	TRADE
CAULK	METAL	SHOWER	TRUCK
CLOG	OVERFLOW	SINK	TUB
DRAIN	PIPES	SIPHON	UNIFORM
FAUCET	PLASTIC	SKILLED	VALVE
FIX	PLUNGER	SNAKE	WASHER
GAS	PRESSURE	SUPPLY	WATER
HAIR	REPAIR	TANK	WRENCH

Solution on page 275

Flea Market

```
D H S Y O T R A D E C I R P
P W T I S J E W E L R Y N E
O F O O V E N D O R K A U R
H H S R O O D T U O V Q E O
S A C G C B H Z S I I T M L
T G B H C I T A N T R T N P
A G R K N R L T N O Z E N X
L L O G A E A A C D W K U E
L E W H S G E F Q E M N F J
B A S K E T K U T R L A S V
W T E V E N T S Q S M L D D
A I J U N K D R E I A B O E
L N Y S T R O L L E N O U C
K G D E S U L Y D B F U Y Y
```

ANTIQUE	CROWD	JEWELRY	STALL
ART	DEALS	JUNK	STROLL
BASKET	EATING	NEW	TOYS
BLANKET	EVENTS	OUTDOORS	TRADE
BOOTH	EXPLORE	PRICE	UNIQUE
BROWSE	FAMILY	RETRO	USED
BUY	FOOD	SALES	VAN
CLOTHING	FUN	SELL	VENDOR
COLLECT	HAGGLE	SHOP	VINTAGE
CRAFTS	HANDMADE	SIT	WALK

Solution on page 275

Frightening

```
G R I F F I N S T A B D F G
W B O A X C K M W F T R L R
N I G L V E K U O H E A O E
I G O L L N I M O D L C W M
E F O E S T N M D E L U E L
T O T N A A G Y E M U L R I
S O E A S U K G N O B A E N
N T L N Q R O O S N R M W T
E A Y G U T N L T S E O G I
K L O E A U G E A X V T H R
N I G L T R Z M K B L N O I
A E R C C L I V E D I A U P
R N A T H G I L N U S H L S
F S G O D Z I L L A O P M I
```

ALIENS	GARGOYLE	SASQUATCH
BATS	GHOUL	SILVER BULLET
BIGFOOT	GODZILLA	SKELETON
CENTAUR	GOLEM	SPIRIT
DEMON	GREMLIN	SUNLIGHT
DEVIL	GRIFFIN	WEREWOLF
DRACULA	IMP	WOODEN STAKE
FALLEN ANGEL	KING KONG	
FRANKENSTEIN	MUMMY	
FREDDY KRUEGER	PHANTOM	

Solution on page 275

132

Women

```
S T E L I M S M G I R L N K
S E C L E L E G A N T J O L
S L A A A S K N A V I D R I
E E L D H E M I G N O R T S
R C N Y G H G R A N D M A A
D A U G H T E R A P A L M C
S R I A H O F A U W I T T Y
T B J V F L I E S U O L B S
P P E S O C K L O V I N G D
T R W W S A E A S E S R U P
A O E A M E C M K N W O G T
B R L T H E C E I N R C N M
S O R S T A H F R P O U O E
N D Y X J Y H S T R A M S L
```

AUNT	ELEGANT	LACE	SALON
BLOUSE	FEMALE	LADY	SANDALS
BOWS	FLOWERS	LOVING	SHE
BRACELET	GIRL	MAKEUP	SILK
CARING	GOWN	MATRON	SKIRT
CLOTHES	GRANDMA	MOM	SMART
DAUGHTER	HAIR	NIECE	SMILE
DIVA	HATS	PRETTY	STRONG
DRESS	HEELS	PROUD	WARM
EARRING	JEWELRY	PURSE	WITTY

Solution on page 275

Haircut

```
C N S T R A I G H T R I A H
S A X P I L C W A V Y R D Z
H I G H L I G H T S W A S H
A C T U C I G N O L E W O T
V I D R E H T A E F O V D K
E T W E R C A E S R E Y A L
L U M S M P S N N Z E N A M
Y A I H R O O R G D A F R O
T E R E E E O T O E S E O H
S B T A B C L R T S P Z L A
N R O R R I M L G A S P O W
I S G N A B Y C O W L I C K
P Z Z U B R A Z O R Y F C X
X S T E L L U M T T R O H S
```

AFRO	CREW	LONG	SHEAR
BANGS	CUT	MANE	SHORT
BARBER	DRY	MIRROR	SNIP
BEAUTICIAN	DYED	MOHAWK	SPLIT ENDS
BUZZ	FEATHER	MULLET	STRAIGHT
CHANGE	FLATTOP	PERM	STYLE
CLIP	GROOMED	RAZOR	TOWEL
COLOR	HAIR	ROLLERS	TRIM
CORNROWS	HIGHLIGHTS	SCISSORS	WASH
COWLICK	LAYERS	SHAVE	WAVY

Solution on page 276

Dishwashing

```
P A N S G R E A S E H S I D
H L A H S A W K C I U Q E S
O S E L B B U B C N N T T Y
T S L I S N E T U A S K A Q
O G C B O W L N O U T R L L
W L U O E S N I R M P S P O
E A P H T O L C H S A W Y A
L S M D E T E R G E N T R D
S S F W N S A N I T I Z E E
A E S A I S U D S F O R K D
U V O T H A N D S B U R C S
C O A E C W O L F R E V O Y
E L K R A P S H S A W E R P
R G C Q M L I F O O D D C O
```

AUTOMATED	FILM	OVERFLOW	SOAK
BOWL	FOOD	PANS	SPARKLE
BUBBLES	FORK	PLATE	SPOON
CLEAN	GLASS	PREWASH	SPRAY
CROCKERY	GLOVES	QUICK WASH	STACK
CRUSTED	GREASE	RINSE	SUDS
CUP	HANDS	SANITIZE	TOWELS
DETERGENT	HOT	SAUCER	UTENSILS
DISHES	LOADED	SCRUB	WASHCLOTH
DRY	MACHINE	SINK	WATER

Solution on page 276

Walk Around

```
P J T W O L S T R I D E Y B
O O D O G S T R E N G T H L
W G G R O U N D P E F N T E
E G F K E X E R C I S E L V
R I R O A D E N T D C M A A
K N F U O R A N E W B E E R
N G U T U T E E E A M V H T
E N N T S S P L L T U O I R
E I A I S S L A S E S M K A
S N D A H N N B T R C A I I
E N L G E C A P R H L L N L
L U M S E E R U S I E L G S
I R S I D E W A L K S G E L
M X F E E T U M M O C K E W
```

BALANCE	GAIT	MILES	SPEED
BRISK	GROUND	MOVEMENT	STRENGTH
COMMUTE	HEALTHY	MUSCLES	STRIDE
DISTANCE	HIKING	NATURE	TRAILS
DOG	JOGGING	PACE	TRAVEL
EXERCISE	KNEES	POWER	WATER
FEET	LEGS	ROAD	WELLNESS
FITNESS	LEISURE	RUNNING	WORKOUT
FOOTPATH	MALL	SIDEWALK	
FUN	MARCHING	SLOW	

Solution on page 276

Chewing Gum

```
S K Y Y H S E R F W A N G I
T C M T E E W S E L B B U B
I A E S I L A R U T A N Y N
C P L A Q U E F N E P V A Y
K Z O T N H R P I E C E O R
C H N R T O B F J S L N N R
U H U A L N M I S C D Y N E
T O E O K U E A G H A T Y B
S R C W H O R D N R T N R U
B S U G A R O T I N E E D C
D E R A U Q S Z V R I D E Y
R O U N D Y G N A T T C A T
S R W R A P P E R B I T E W
T N I M Y B O H C I T R U S
```

BAZOOKA	CLEAN	MELON	STICK
BERRY	COLORFUL	MINT	STUCK
BIG RED	CRAVINGS	NATURAL	SUGAR
BITE	CUBE	PACK	SWEET
BREATH	DENTYNE	PIECE	TANGY
BUBBLES	DRY	PLAQUE	TASTY
CANDY	FLAVOR	ROUND	TEETH
CHEW	FRESH	SORGHUM	TRIDENT
CINNAMON	FRUITY	SOUR	WAD
CITRUS	GNAW	SQUARE	WRAPPER

Solution on page 276

Environment

```
R T R A C T H S V S N O W R
L A S E K A L L N A E C O E
Y K I C G U H A F O L U S H
Y L A N L I R M O X Y L L N
I T G R S I O I R K F N E B
P U R E D E M N E E L T A Y
A R E A U N C A S S O R V C
T R E G O P U T T R R E E L
J U N G L E M T S E A S S E
G E R A C W S E N V M E E A
R H N F O D O M A I N D E N
A T S O R E V I R D X R R U
S S D I Z N E G Y X O G T A
S S B I F O Z R E T A W V F
```

ANIMALS	FAUNA	MEADOW	TRACT
AREA	FISH	OCEAN	TREES
BARREN	FLORA	OXYGEN	TUNDRA
BIRDS	FORESTS	OZONE	TURF
CANYON	GRASS	PLANTS	VALLEY
CLEAN	GREEN	PURE	WATER
CLIMATE	INSECTS	RAIN	WOODS
CLOUDS	JUNGLE	REGION	
DESERT	LAKES	RIVER	
DIVERSE	LEAVES	SKY	
DOMAIN	LUSH	SNOW	

Solution on page 277

Types of Music

```
N B G R U N G E J R R S S L
O W L U O S D V I A D P R A
R V O N F C L I G D O I E C
C U H T E Q K T S P N R G I
H H A E O W I A U C L I N S
E Y R I L M O N B A O T I S
S A D I E E K R T I J U S A
T W R P S R C E L P L A G L
R D O E O T M T K E R L Z C
A A C C C Y I L R G A S Y Z
T O K P V O O A E O J N A B
I R B A H F R U N E N B S C
U B E B O P L D F U S I O N
G H D N A B G I B D A N C E
```

ALTERNATIVE

BANJO

BEBOP

BIG BAND

BLUEGRASS

BROADWAY

CHRISTIAN

CLASSICAL

DANCE

DISCO

ELECTRONIC

FOLK

FUSION

GRUNGE

GUITAR

HARD ROCK

HEAVY METAL

INDIE

JAZZ

MOTOWN

NEW ORLEANS

ORCHESTRA

POP

PUNK ROCK

RAGTIME

RECORD

ROCKABILLY

SINGERS

SOUL

SPIRITUALS

Solution on page 277

Apparel

```
Q M X O T R I H S K I R T M
T G E T U P A S C O T L E B
E H S A S T D L H L C O A T
K R R N S T F G L O R K M E
C A C E C U N I F O R M S S
A E V A A I D A T C C T W U
J W C J R D E S P L Q E S O
E T G E F D S T O O A P K L
P O V A X E I T J T S A C B
A O H Q R U G G E H N J A R
C F O D S M N R A I O A L O
C O S T U M E T N N L M S B
O D E X U T R N S G Y A W E
G O W N R M I T T E N S T J
```

ASCOT	DESIGNER	MITTENS	SKIRT
BELT	DRESS	NYLONS	SLACKS
BLOUSE	FOOTWEAR	OUTFIT	SOCKS
CAPE	GARMENT	PAJAMAS	SUIT
CARDIGAN	GETUP	PANTS	SWEATER
CLOTHING	GOWN	ROBE	THREADS
COAT	HAT	SASH	TIE
COLLAR	HOSE	SCARF	TUXEDO
COSTUME	JACKET	SHIRT	UNIFORM
COVERING	JEANS	SHORTS	VEST

Solution on page 277

Happy Things

```
S I U S N W O L C E L I M S
P E T S E Z I R P T O Y S Q
J Y S S T I L O V E C P S U
G L W S T G N I R P S P D C
P I C N I C S O C B L U I A
A M G F K K E W P A H P K R
R A T G U H A F Y B T F M D
K F W F L N K I C I R C U S
S A F R I E N D S E I O S M
N S E M A G S Y E S B M I O
U D A N C I N G D O S E C O
F L O W E R S S I N T D A R
S N U S S E C E R G A Y K G
F V H E J J O Y B H H C E T
```

ANIMALS	DANCING	HUG	PLAYING
BABIES	FAMILY	JOY	PONIES
BIRTH	FLOWERS	KIDS	PRIZES
BRIDES	FRIENDS	KISSES	PUPPY
CAKE	FUN	KITTEN	RECESS
CANDY	GAMES	LOVE	SMILE
CARDS	GIFT	MUSIC	SONG
CIRCUS	GIGGLES	PARKS	SPRING
CLOWN	GROOMS	PETS	SUN
COMEDY	HATS	PICNICS	TOYS

Solution on page 277

It's Genetic

```
B Y A R E C E S S I V E S S
O G M G D V A R I A T I O N
D O I G O G N I R P S F F O
Y L N E C N A T I R E H N I
D O O E C N E I C S M S U T
I I A V I C E L L S O T C A
S B C O T R A I T S S U L T
O X I L E H E L B U O D E U
R D D U N L S P E R M Y O M
D W S T E Y E C O L O R T O
E H E I G H T L N N R D I T
R N A O N E R D L I H C D H
P H E N O T Y P E A C W E E
A N D M O R G A N I S M S R
```

ALLELE	EGG	ORGANISMS
AMINO ACIDS	EVOLUTION	PHENOTYPE
BIOLOGY	EYE COLOR	RECESSIVE
BODY	GENETIC CODE	RNA
CELLS	HEIGHT	SCIENCE
CHILDREN	INHERITANCE	SPERM
CHROMOSOMES	MOTHER	STUDY
DISORDER	MUTATIONS	TRAITS
DNA	NUCLEOTIDES	VARIATION
DOUBLE HELIX	OFFSPRING	

Solution on page 278

Fish Tank

```
R B U B B L E S E L B R A M
H E A T E R S S E L B B E P
S R Z L A M P S R E F F U P
E E N I R A M C O O L I N G
R N C G N K L O A C H S I F
F P I H S O K S O S T A N D
P A L T M U I R A U Q A E I
G S Y S R Q T E S T K I T S
Y S R T T O R N D S P M U P
P A C E E A G A G R A V E L
P L A N T S S E L T R U T A
U G E E R L E L N M O L L Y
G A O E A C I C H L I D A X
R E V O C Y S F R O G S S J
```

ACRYLIC	DISPLAY	LAMP	PUFFERS
AERATE	EEL	LIGHTS	PUMPS
ALGAE	FILTER	LOACH	SALT
AQUARIUM	FISH	MARBLES	SEA HORSE
BUBBLES	FRESH	MARINE	SHIP
CICHLID	FROGS	MOLLY	STAND
CLEANERS	GLASS	NETS	TEST KITS
COOLING	GRAVEL	NITROGEN	TETRA
COVER	GUPPY	PEBBLES	TURTLES
DEIONIZER	HEATER	PLANTS	

Solution on page 278

Keeping Clean

```
N P Y T E F A S P T A E W S
O E G S B A W S U O R A L S
I M O O R H T A B I S C K E
T I L L N E S S L L A I H E
N B O D Y H Y G I E N E A C
E D I S I N F E C T I O N N
V G M O R L T O H P T D D A
E N E O X I U E E A A A W R
R I D P I H A B A P T I A A
P N I M C L U H L E I L S E
A A P A T R T R T R O Y H P
O E E H C L O T H I N G I P
S L Y S C I T O I B I T N A
B C L E A N L I N E S S G L
```

ANTIBIOTICS
APPEARANCE
BATHROOM
BLEACH
BODY HYGIENE
CLEANING
CLEANLINESS
CLOTHING
DAILY
DISINFECTION

EPIDEMIOLOGY
HAIR
HAND WASHING
HEALTHY
ILLNESS
ORAL
PREVENTION
PUBLIC HEALTH
SAFETY
SANITATION

SCRUB
SHAMPOO
SKIN
SOAP
SWABS
SWEAT
TOILET PAPER

Solution on page 278

Thanksgiving Dinner

```
Y T L F N F R I E N D S S L
E V R A C G R A C E T A L G
K B P M N O V E N U L A T G
R R D I N I N G F A B G S A
U E T L O O U F D T N N A T
T A T Y B E I R O R S I O H
E D F H S N E O O E J L R E
N E S T G S F C O B B L E R
I I S V S U M T H O T I T S
W P G I Z Z A R D S R F T T
P I N R U T H L S M A Y U E
Z G Y N O I T A C A V U B E
N I K P M U P N A C E P Q W
V I S I T P U O S L L O R S
```

BREAD	FOOTBALL	OVEN	STUFFING
BUTTER	FRIENDS	PECAN	SWEETS
CARVE	GATHER	PIE	TRAVEL
COBBLER	GIZZARDS	POTATOES	TURKEY
CORN	GRACE	PUMPKIN	TURNIP
DINING	GUESTS	ROAST	VACATION
DRESSING	HAM	ROLLS	VISIT
EATING	HOT	SALAD	WINE
FAMILY	LAUGHTER	SOUP	WISHBONE
FILLING	NAP	SQUASH	YAMS

Solution on page 278

Computer Programs

```
T N E L N G W C O M P A N Y
N O R D I O N R E S W O R B
E I U C U N I I I W I U H N
M T G Z A C U T G T N T S E
P A I L L L A X A A E I A X
O C F U K A C T B M M L R E
L I N E S E N U I U O I C C
E L O E D E S G L O G T O U
V P C O M I C A U A N Y U T
E P C U N A T I D A T A D A
D A C E D I G I F W G E L B
M O S R O R R E N F A E E L
D S G N I M M A R G O R P E
T E E H S D A E R P S L E U
```

ADWARE	DATA	LINUX
APPLICATION	DEVELOPMENT	OFFICE SUITE
AUTOMATION	DOCUMENTATION	PROGRAMMING
BROWSER	EDITING	RUN
BUSINESS	EDUCATIONAL	SIMULATION
CALCULATE	ERRORS	SPREADSHEET
CODE	EXECUTABLE	UTILITY
COMPANY	GAME	WRITE
CONFIGURE	IMAGING	
CRASH	LANGUAGE	

Solution on page 279

Bank on It

```
Y P Q W N A T I O N A L E G
M S A B I L L S I L C T G T
O N N Y A F I N A N C I A L
N I I W M L T W S L O D G A
O O N C A E A D E S U E T T
C C V F R R N N M E N R R I
E U E E D O D T C Y T C O P
C A S H B I A R E E S A M A
J T T T N Y C N E R R U C C
F I M G O V O L A V A U L T
W U E Z L M S T I S O P E D
L G N I K C E H C N A R B E
I N T D Y T I R U C E S W B
F E E S S E N I S U B S H T
```

ACCOUNTS	COINS	FUNDS	RATE
ATMS	CREDIT	INTEREST	SECURITY
BALANCE	CURRENCY	INVESTMENT	VAULT
BILLS	CUSTOMERS	LENDING	WITHDRAWAL
BONDS	DEBT	LINES	
BRANCH	DEPOSITS	MONEY	
BUSINESS	ECONOMY	MORTGAGE	
CAPITAL	FDIC	NATIONAL	
CASH	FEES	OVERDRAWN	
CHECKING	FINANCIAL	PAYMENT	

Solution on page 279

Driving a Car

```
F T R A V E L L M R E G C A
S E R I T L I Y L I G H T O
L A N G I S C A E R R M P I
E H O R N H E W G K E R A D
E K G Q C I N E S G T V O A
H K R T D G S V E Y U R E R
W S U A S H E I L E M I S L
T L E B P W E R U N M D D R
C A L U I A N D R R O E E E
S D A O R Y G Y O U C T E E
N E O F T W I N D O W S P T
R P M O V I N G O J R P S S
U B T A E S E G U A G E A R
T O U R B O N K N U R T I M
```

BELT	GUIDE	MIRROR	SPEED
CLUTCH	HIGHWAY	MOVING	STEER
COMMUTE	HORN	PARK	TIRES
CRUISING	JOURNEY	PEDALS	TOUR
DOOR	KEY	RADIO	TRAVEL
DRIVEWAY	KNOB	RIDE	TRIPS
ENGINE	LEVER	ROADS	TRUNK
GAUGES	LICENSE	RULES	TURNS
GEAR	LIGHT	SEAT	WHEELS
GRILL	MAP	SIGNAL	WINDOWS

Solution on page 279

Solar Power

```
L E N A P M I R R O R P D B
T B Y G R E N E W A B L E A
S H A G L E V L C Q N A S L
M T I T O T U I A A M N E T
E R T R T L C S T M P T R E
T A R V A E O U A N R S T R
S E A O L D R N E B E E A N
Y G C L T A I I H U L C H A
S A K T L C X A E C S E N T
E R I A T N E M T S E V N I
S O N G N A E L C I M T E V
N T G E R U T U F O O R E E
E S A T E L L I T E H N R B
L I G H T C O N V E R T G Q
```

ALTERNATIVE	FUTURE	PANEL	SUN
BATTERIES	GREEN	PLANTS	SYSTEMS
BEAM	HEAT	RADIATION	TECHNOLOGY
CAR	HOMES	REFLECTOR	THERMAL
CELL	INCENTIVE	RENEWABLE	TRACKING
CLEAN	INVESTMENT	REUSABLE	VOLTAGE
CONVERT	LENSES	ROOF	
DESERT	LIGHT	SATELLITE	
EARTH	MIRROR	SPACE	
ENERGY	NATURAL	STORAGE	

Solution on page 279

Collecting Things

```
E C I R P P A T C H E S Y R
C O M P I L E S R E T S O P
A M S R G G Y A L P S I D P
C I S E N I R U G I F N F I
Q C T S I R O T C E L L O C
U S N E T L B O O K S K S T
I Y E R N M F G T B E N S U
R R M V U O M R F O U O I R
E L A E H D I A E T Q I L E
H E N D S N N P A T I T S S
T W R U K A T H M L T C Q T
A E O E F F C S A E N U R O
G J T E L B M E S S A A B R
O S T C E S N I S N I O C E
```

ACQUIRE
AMASS
ANTIQUES
ART
ASSEMBLE
AUCTION
AUTOGRAPHS
BOOKS
BOTTLES

BUTTERFLIES
CASE
COINS
COLLECTOR
COMICS
COMPILE
DISPLAY
FANDOM
FIGURINES

FOSSILS
FUN
GATHER
GET
HUNTING
INSECTS
JEWELRY
MINT
ORNAMENTS

PATCHES
PICTURES
POSTERS
PRESERVED
PRICE
RESTORE
TRINKETS

Solution on page 280

Pests

```
U G N A T R E G G I H C D R
G U B K N I T S L B C R M O
E B I F I R E F L Y A M K T
T Y M R O W W O L G O F A A
I D T S E I L F O S R B T D
M A E G G S E N Q U K T Y E
R L N M K S F U I L C H D R
E C R R R L I T G R O I I P
T O O O Y T F N I U C U D F
S B H W O L B C S I B I S L
U W Y L Y I K E T E H D P E
C E E A T E F S D P C T E A
O B E E T L E P A R T T O B
L S S M Y P I L L B U G S M
```

APHID	EGGS	HOUSEFLY	PESTICIDE
BEDBUG	FIREFLY	INSECTS	PILL BUG
BEETLE	FLEA	KATYDID	PREDATOR
BITES	FLIES	LADYBUG	STINKBUG
CHIGGER	FRUIT FLY	LOCUST	TERMITE
COBWEB	GLOWWORM	LOUSE	TRAP
COCKROACH	GNAT	MEALWORM	WEBS
CRICKET	HORNET	MOSQUITO	
DRAGONFLY	HORSEFLY	MOTH	

Solution on page 280

Brewing Beer

```
N N S J E F L S P O H E A T
P D B T L K I E T U O T S S
S A T A A C O P P E R P M A
O R V S R O B R E C I P E E
U O R T I L A G E R N Z L Y
R M E E T R E A N M F B L P
G A T L T I G Y Z H U A O S
F D T C E A K Z Y S S T S W
D G I N F M W W M A I C U E
T R B U E D A M E M O H G E
R A A R Q M A R S R N J A T
A I N F S I R E A M B E R D
T N B O T T L E M C A S K M
K E G X I N W I F I L T E R
```

AIR LOCK	CARAMEL	HEAT	RECIPE
ALE	CASK	HOMEMADE	SMELL
AMBER	COPPER	HOPS	SOUR
AROMA	DRAFT	INFUSION	STOUT
BARLEY	ENZYMES	KEG	SUGAR
BATCH	FERMENT	LAGER	SWEET
BITTER	FILTER	LIQUID	TART
BOIL	FLAVOR	MASH	TASTE
BOTTLE	GRAIN	MEAD	WATER
BREW KIT	GRIST	POT	YEAST

Solution on page 280

Get Published

```
S L A N R U O J L A G E L I
U E D T E N R E T N I T S A
T V V U P U B L I S H E R G
P O A B E S T S E L L E R E
I N N C V B I N D I N G G N
R K C O Y T C O N T R A C T
C C E V R G N I T E K R A M
S A L E S T H G I R Y P O C
U B V R N E W S P A P E R S
N D M P R O D U C T I O N G
A R T I C L E S M U S I C O
M A B O O K S T O R E A Q L
J H M A G A Z I N E S H W B
P A P E R B A C K A I D E M
```

ADVANCE	COVER	MUSIC
ADVERTISING	HARDBACK	NEWSPAPERS
AGENT	INTERNET	NOVEL
ARTICLES	JOURNALS	PAPERBACK
BESTSELLER	LEGAL	PRODUCTION
BINDING	LITERATURE	PUBLISHER
BLOGS	MAGAZINES	SALES
BOOKSTORE	MANUSCRIPT	
CONTRACT	MARKETING	
COPYRIGHT	MEDIA	

Solution on page 280

Tax Time

```
E T A L D E D U C T I O N P
C A T L E X E M P T I O N C
G X N A E X T E N S I O N R
S P E N A L T I E S T A T E
R A M O F X N R U T E R A D
E Y Y S G I R F S E G A W I
B E A R N I N G S S O R G T
M R P E G O P A Y S T U B S
U W T P C S I G N A T U R E
N P R O P E R T Y C D I N S
M K R O W R E P A P I B E M
A Q R E P O R T I N G A I R
I N C O M E V A S I O N L O
L P A Y R O L L A R E D E F
```

ASSETS	FEDERAL	NET	REPORTING
CONFUSION	FINANCIAL	NUMBERS	RETURN
CREDITS	FORMS	PAPERWORK	SIGNATURE
DEDUCTION	GROSS	PAYMENT	STATE
DONATIONS	INCOME	PAYROLL	TAXPAYER
EARNINGS	IRS	PAYSTUBS	WAGES
EVASION	LATE	PENALTIES	
EXEMPTION	LIEN	PERSONAL	
EXTENSION	MAIL	PROPERTY	

Solution on page 281

Made of Wood

```
S E X O B B E D P O S T T S
R E S U O H H I I T A E D S
E S L W O B N R A B N N H D
S D E S K O C I L I I E G N
S R I K C H R L B W L G U A
E A G C A S A A D F S Y O T
R T H I S B C O A S T E R S
D I R T E L O P M E T O T V
O U B S T W P O R C H E S T
O G A M E C N E F R A M E S
W B F U R N I T U R E M T I
Y E K R O W T R A I L I N G
L B P D N U O R G Y A L P N
P A D D L E O N A C L O C K
```

ARTWORK	CHAIR	FURNITURE	SHELF
BARN	CHEST	GUITAR	SIGN
BASEBALL BAT	CLOCK	HOUSE	SLEIGH
BEDPOST	COASTERS	PADDLE	STAIRS
BOOKCASE	DESK	PINOCCHIO	TOTEM POLE
BOWL	DRESSER	PLAYGROUND	TOYS
BOXES	DRUMSTICKS	PLYWOOD	TROUGH
CABINET	FENCE	PORCH	TV STAND
CANOE	FRAME	RAILING	WOODWINDS

Solution on page 281

The Olympic Games

```
F L A M E D I W D L R O W E
C O A C H E S D S L U I O C
B N T D E W L L C A E D G E
E D H E E D A E I B Y L N E
I O L C B M D I T Y N B I R
J N E A A E E F S E O A M G
I S T T D E M Z A L H S M N
N C I H M T D S N L T K I I
G O C L I T L G M O A E W N
N U S O N I O N Y V R T S I
I N U N T M G I G M A B M A
V T Y N O M E R E C M A A R
I R X F N O I S I V E L E T
D Y R E H C R A T N A L T A
```

ARCHERY
ATHLETICS
ATLANTA
BADMINTON
BASKETBALL
BEIJING
BRONZE MEDAL
CEREMONY
COACHES
COMMITTEE

COUNTRY
DECATHLON
DIVING
FIELD
FLAME
GOLD MEDAL
GREECE
GYMNASTICS
IOC
LONDON

MARATHON
MEDALS
RINGS
SWIMMING
TEAMS
TELEVISION
TRAINING
VOLLEYBALL
WORLDWIDE

Solution on page 281

Symphony Orchestra

```
E G A T S T E P M U R T B V
H C A B N Y S O U N D S I D
N R E D O M M I S E T O N V
A O N A I P R T L C L A O R
H C S H T A U E O A B E I O
Y A O B C N E N S L C N T M
M D L U E I C I T O U O A A
O R O L S E N R R V P B V N
Z H I L R T E A I E C M O T
A Y S T E F I L N L I O O I
R T T E N M D C G Y S R S C
T H C H O R U S S S U T O E
E M E H T B A H A R M O N Y
C E L L O Q O B R A S S G S
```

ACOUSTICS
AUDIENCE
BACH
BAND
BASSOON
BRASS
CELLO
CHORUS
CLARINET
COMPOSER

CONCERT
HALL
HARMONY
LOVELY
MELODY
MODERN
MOZART
MUSIC
NOTES
OBOE

OVATION
PIANO
RHYTHM
ROMANTIC
SECTIONS
SOLOIST
SONG
SOUNDS
STAGE
STRINGS

THEME
TONE
TROMBONE
TRUMPET
TUNE
TYMPANI
VIOLA
VOCALIST

Solution on page 281

Media

```
R O H C N A C O V E R A G E
P P U B L I C I T Y X W N N
A S T R I N G E R G N J I I
M A R K E T I N G O R O P Z
P F A E D E H S I L B U P A
H F T L I R T S O O O R I G
L I I B T N S E N N O N L A
E L N A O E O C L H K A C M
T I G C R T C N I C S L C O
N A S P A S I E N E I I N V
I T X X W U A I E T V T F I
R E X E N I L D A E H W R E
P S N U L E R U S O P X E A
N O I T A T S A C D A O R B
```

AFFILIATES	EXPOSURE	PAMPHLET
ANCHOR	EXPRESSION	PRINT
ARTICLE	HEADLINE	PUBLICITY
AUDIENCES	INTERNET	PUBLISHED
BOOKS	JOURNAL	RATINGS
BROADCAST	MAGAZINE	SOCIAL
CABLE	MARKETING	STATION
CLIPPING	MOVIE	STRINGER
COVERAGE	NEWS	TECHNOLOGY
EDITOR	ONLINE	WEB

Solution on page 282

True Friends

```
D O O H D L I H C F G W D E
E E A T T A C H M E N T W M
M V C C O M R A D E S H I P
O I T N X X L S W L Y H C A
T T I O A Y A S A I M O L T
I R V I J T P O T N P N O H
O O I T I I N C T G A E S Y
N P T C D N E I R F T S E B
A P I E E I P A A P H T N U
L U E F E F L T C U Y Y E D
K S S F N F E I T C Q K S D
R C Z A G A H O I R O C S I
G U E G N I D N O B U R A E
O X T N A D I F N O C E D S
```

ACCORD
ACQUAINTANCE
ACTIVITIES
AFFECTION
AFFINITY
ASSOCIATION
ATTACHMENT
ATTRACTION
BEST FRIEND
BONDING

BUDDIES
CHILDHOOD
CLOSENESS
COMRADESHIP
CONFIDANT
EMOTIONAL
EMPATHY
FEELING
HELP
HONESTY

NEED
PEN PAL
SUPPORTIVE
SYMPATHY
TRUE

Solution on page 282

Take a Taxi

```
T R I P O Y P S E I T I C W
Y E N O M I L E A G E A A E
H L L A C B D E S X B V G C
L T W K F A L A P D E A C I
E I U L J C G E R D G I A V
V P A S I K N I I G F L B R
A G M H R S V S U F T A B E
R P E A I E T L A A S B I S
T V T V R A V R X R T L E H
H E E S N T T I O E E E R A
G Y R C A T C H R P E U I R
I N E W Y O R K U D R F H E
L N O D N O L O C A T I O N
R I D E U F D N A T S K A Q
```

AIRPORTS	EXPENSIVE	LUGGAGE	SHARE
AVAILABLE	FARE	METER	STAND
BACKSEAT	FLAG	MILEAGE	STREETS
CAB DRIVER	FUEL	MONEY	TAXI
CABBIE	GAS	NEW YORK	TIP
CALL	HAIL	PICK UP	TRAFFIC
CATCH	HIRE	RADIO	TRAVEL
CITIES	LIGHT	RATE	TRIP
DISTANCE	LOCATION	RIDE	VEHICLE
DRIVERS	LONDON	SERVICE	WAVE

Solution on page 282

Relaxing

```
P Z C O M F O R T N A P S B
O F O R Y G N I D A E R E H
O P G N U N O S S I L B M S
L K N E S I C R E X E G A D
G U I C T R S A I L I N G N
S N K K A O F I R E S I D E
D H I U E L W I N E U P M I
S I B T R O M G S G R M A R
E K V R T C D N N H E A S F
S I I E E I S I E I I C S C
A N V I R A S K N S T N A O
E G S O N T K O P N S S G Z
Y O G A M G Y O J N E Q E Y
B K O O B E A C H P A R K R
```

BEACH	COZY	GAMES	RETREAT
BIKING	CRUISING	HIKING	SAILING
BLISS	DINNER	LEISURE	SITTING
BOOK	DIVERT	MASSAGE	SKIING
BREAK	EASE	MOVIE	SUNNY
CALMNESS	ENJOY	NAPS	WINE
CAMPING	EXERCISE	PARK	YOGA
COLORING	FIRESIDE	POOL	
COMFORT	FISHING	READING	
COOKING	FRIENDS	RESTING	

Solution on page 282

Father

```
H F C I O R E H T N E R A P
U U E N I L P I C S I D N A
G N I V I G R O F K K R E T
S R O L E M O D E L A C R I
L D H E R I T A G E H O D E
O D E T O V E D L C T N L N
Y D O T S U C Y R S G C I T
A P A P C R T A E G N E H C
L L I R G E I C K N E R C E
T P A T E R N A L I R N A P
Y M A N T A G N O R T S O S
R E L A T I V E O A S P C E
Y P P A H G N I H C A E T R
E V O L D E D N O B R A V E
```

ANCESTOR	DEVOTED	LOVE	RELATIVE
BONDED	DISCIPLINE	LOYALTY	RESPECT
BRAVE	FORGIVING	MAN	ROLE MODEL
CARING	FUN	PAPA	STRENGTH
CHILDREN	GRILL	PARENT	STRONG
COACH	HAPPY	PATERNAL	TEACHING
CONCERN	HERITAGE	PATIENT	
CONNECTED	HEROIC	PATRIARCH	
CUSTODY	HUGS	POP	
DAD	LEARN	PROTECTING	

Solution on page 283

Battery-Powered

```
Y S L O O T L D C A M E R A
R L D S C I N O R T C E L E
U L E A T C I E A I Y N S L
C E Z H U D O L R A L M D E
R C I K A T K M L R O L I C
E U G R C A O P P K U R A T
M A R T L O D M E U E C G R
O N E I O V L A O T T G N I
T R N K D Y L C O B W E I C
E E E L B A S O P S I D R C
S T S T R A C F L O G L A A
H N F M U S I C P L A Y E R
L A P T O P L A C I M E H C
N L C H A R G E T A B L E T
```

ALKALINE	DRILL	LITHIUM
AUTOMOBILE	DVD PLAYER	MERCURY
CAMERA	ELECTRIC CAR	MUSIC PLAYER
CELLS	ELECTRONICS	RADIO
CHARGE	ENERGIZED	REMOTE
CHEMICAL	FAN	SCOOTER
CLOCK	GOLF CART	SMOKE ALARM
COMPUTER	HEARING AID	TABLET
CURRENT	LANTERN	TOOLS
DISPOSABLE	LAPTOP	TOYS

Solution on page 283

Aerospace

```
N E T F E N I G N E C A P S
O B C I U S O E O L L O P A
O S O N P S O T S T A E H E
M H S O E K E L S P D A Y Y
I U N T S I C L A U I Y S R
S T G O E T C O A R O L I T
S T L A I N E S C G R H C N
I L A E L T A R O V E R S E
O E O R U A A L T I T U D E
N U S R S F X I P G S K N R
M I L I T A R Y V R A N U L
I M A G I N G G R A V I T Y
C O M E T N O I T I N G I W
P R E S E A R C H C N U A L
```

AIRCRAFT	ECLIPSE	IMAGING	RESEARCH
ALTITUDE	ENGINE	LAUNCH	ROVERS
APOLLO	FUEL	LUNAR	SCIENCE
ASTEROID	FUSELAGE	MILITARY	SHUTTLE
AVIATION	GALAXY	MISSION	SOLAR
BOOSTER	GRAVITY	MOON	SPACE
COCKPIT	HEAT	PHYSICS	STARS
COMET	HOUSTON	PLANETS	SUN
CONTROLS	IGNITION	REENTRY	

Solution on page 283

Math

```
D E C I M A L U M R O F A E
D P O N U M B E R S E T S Q
A U M E T N E G N A T F U U
S O P G L C C L R Y R O S A
E R U A A N I I P A T U R L
L G T T R E T N C I L A A S
G R E I E H S T E U T R O G
N A V V M I I N C I E L L E
A P I E U O T L O A V P U O
B H T X N Y A R B E G L A M
A I I M E C T N E N O P X E
C N S N U O S E R U G I F T
U G O C O S I N E M I R P R
S M P R O D U C T N U O C Y
```

ABACUS
ADD
ALGEBRA
ANGLES
AREA
ARITHMETIC
CALCULUS
COMPUTE
COSINE

COUNT
DECIMAL
EQUALS
EXPONENT
FIGURES
FORMULA
FRACTION
GEOMETRY
GRAPHING

GROUP
MONEY
MULTIPLE
NEGATIVE
NUMBERS
NUMERAL
POSITIVE
PRIME
PRODUCT

QUOTIENT
RATIO
ROOT
SETS
SOLVE
STATISTIC
SUM
TANGENT

Solution on page 283

Navigating

```
D G N I Y L F Z S R S N S T
E E V E H I C L E D O F R R
E N A L P B N E X I U U A A
L N C D A N T S T S T T T V
O I T F R S O A A T H A S E
R A G N G E N I N A P O P L
T T H H O I C L T N O B I A
N P T T T I S K R C L E L T
O A S S R H T P O E E A O I
C C E T A O O A I N L R T T
E D W L C E N U C H I I I U
A J D E G R E E S O S N N D
N L O N G I T U D E L G G E
S T R A H C O M P A S S P G
```

BEARINGS	DISTANCE	PLANE
BOAT	EAST	ROUTE
CAPTAIN	FLYING	SAIL
CARTOGRAPHY	GPS	SEXTANT
CHARTS	LATITUDE	SHIPS
COMPASS	LIGHTHOUSE	SOUTH POLE
CONTROL	LOCATION	STARS
DEAD RECKONING	LONGITUDE	STEER
DEGREES	NORTH	TRAVEL
DESTINATION	OCEAN	VEHICLE
DIRECTION	PILOTING	WEST

Solution on page 284

Jump in the Pool

```
J U M P S P A L F S P A K S
S C P E C C S U N S H I N E
B O A E L H N M T J C R D L
R U R L G D L R E K V B O G
A R T Y A N O O B D J O L G
C S Y T M K P O R S C R Y O
E E T S E S A A N I H N M G
T W I E S R U I D S N E P K
A E U E D G F B A D E E I T
N T S R E L E L M T L C C R
S A M F I D P P Y E K E P E
Y O I P I S D N E I R F A A
O L W L B I K I N I O G C D
T F S E V A W G A W A T E R
```

AIRBORNE	FREESTYLE	NOODLE	SWIMSUIT
BIKINI	FRIENDS	OLYMPIC	TANS
BUTTERFLY	FUN	PACE	TOYS
CAP	GAMES	PADDLE	TREAD
CHLORINE	GOGGLES	PARTY	WATER
COOL	JUMP	RACE	WAVES
COURSE	KICKBOARD	SLIDE	WET
DIP	KICKING	SPLASH	
FINS	LAPS	STROKE	
FLIP	LIFEGUARD	SUBMERGE	
FLOAT	MEET	SUNSHINE	

Solution on page 284

Fast Things

```
M O T O R B O A T E J J S L
A N O C L A F A S T B A L L
C N W E E X P R E S S G E A
H A I R P L A N E V J U D B
S L N A M R E P U S R A C E
P A D N R J R E T N I R P S
E C T M O T O R C Y C L E A
E H S E D N U O H Y E R G B
D A L E L I B O M W O N S B
B T I D A L W A V E M I T U
O E G N H S I F L I A S N L
A E H U V A N T E L O P E L
T H T O F P E R E G R I N E
A C V S S P A C E S H I P T
```

AIRPLANE	FASTBALL	SAILFISH	TIDAL WAVE
ANTELOPE	GREYHOUND	SATELLITES	TIME
BASEBALL	JAGUAR	SLED	TRAIN
BULLET	JET	SNOWMOBILE	WIND
CANNONBALL	LIGHT	SOUND	
CARS	MACH SPEED	SPACESHIP	
CHEETAH	MOTORBOAT	SPEEDBOAT	
EXPRESS	MOTORCYCLE	SPRINTER	
FALCON	PEREGRINE	SUPERMAN	

Solution on page 284

Electrician

```
P O S I T I V E R E P M A L
S T T S Q U V R M L R R G R
A R L E E I O U I O Q E P E
Y A O G T L N K Y A A K O P
G I V A N I E S C D P A W P
R N G T M I B R R A P E E O
E E E U L P R R I E L R R C
N D L O I S L I O W I B E U
E A B U G E P I W W A L X R
M C A T H C X A F A N T P R
G O C L T I U C R I C O T E
Z V S E R V I C E K E C U N
K E T T J E B A T T E R Y T
G R O U N D E L L I K S N V
```

ALUMINUM	CIRCUIT	LOAD	SKILLED
AMPERE	COPPER	NEGATIVE	SPARK
AMPLIFIER	COVER	OUTAGE	TRAINED
APPLIANCE	CURRENT	OUTLET	VOLTS
BATTERY	DEVICES	PLIERS	WATT
BLACKOUT	ENERGY	POSITIVE	WIRELESS
BREAKER	FAN	POWER	WIRING
BROWNOUT	GROUND	REPAIR	
CABLE	LIGHT	SERVICE	

Solution on page 284

Monosyllabic Words

```
Z G X N K S M C A R J F N G
A S D W O W U M I H R O C K
Z D N E O D P G N N E G B E
N Z Z P E M B G Q O N R J Z
Q W A J U N K G K M T A O B
B M S J A X A R O O B L U E
Y T Y T S Q U V O O T I W A
Y U I A B A Z H O G I J I T
B Q T U L I N K T W E R G G
N U S D N U G D I U W O N O
Z O V W K I A A O T L O D H
K Y Q S D C X Y U G E F I L
S F Y Y G A V D P Y I I G B
Y G V A E L T T M R A G I P
```

BEAT	FOG	KITE	ROCK
BIG	GOO	LIFE	ROOF
BLUE	HER	LINK	SAND
BOAT	HIM	LOG	STY
BOOK	HOG	MOO	SUN
BUS	JAZZ	NEED	TOO
DAY	JIG	NOW	VOW
DIG	JOB	PIG	WIG
DOG	JUMP	RENT	WOW
FIG	JUNK	RIG	YOU

Solution on page 285

Acting

```
S Y W R A P R O D U C E R E U
U A C A S T I N G D E A Y C
O L W T R M N S S R L W E N
M P Z S P D A E E A E A M A
A E U R E R R U G M B R U M
F I O E R R G O D A R D T O
G V S H K O O P B I I M S R
E O G E L A T C A E T L O E
S M N A T Q M C N R Y I C S
T P I R C S C C E E T F O E
U D K S V E E S C R E E N N
R W O E N L I G H T I N G E
E M O T I O N C O M E D Y C
C B B T H E A T E R A C T S
```

ACCENT	COSTUME	LIGHTING	SCRIPT
ACTS	DIALOGUE	MAKEUP	SETS
AGENT	DIRECTOR	MOVIE	STAR
AUDIENCE	DRAMA	PART	THEATER
AUDITION	EMOTION	PLAY	WARDROBE
AWARD	ENCORE	PRODUCER	WRAP
BOOKING	FAMOUS	REHEARSE	
CASTING	FILM	ROMANCE	
CELEBRITY	GESTURE	SCENES	
COMEDY	IMPROVE	SCREEN	

Solution on page 285

Sites of the World

```
E N B P E T R A T O S L O Y
M N G D A N U B E R I V E R
A S A N T A R C T I C A G E
D Q Z E B E R L I N P F D M
E U O M C C A I R O R F I M
R A M A Z O N R I V E R R A
T W O D M C N S C O W O B H
O V U R U I E A R A T K R E
N A N E N T B P I N N G E L
A L T V I C G P M D A N W L
G L F O C R I O E E N A O I
A E U O H A B R A S S I T L
N Y J H U D S O N B A Y X O
T R I L A H A M J A T S S B
```

AMAZON RIVER	CRIMEA	NOTRE DAME
ANDES	DANUBE RIVER	OSLO
ANGKOR	HOOVER DAM	PETRA
ANTARCTICA	HUDSON BAY	SAPPORO
ANTWERP	INDIAN OCEAN	SQUAW VALLEY
ARCTIC OCEAN	LILLEHAMMER	TAJ MAHAL
BERLIN	MOUNT FUJI	TOWER BRIDGE
BIG BEN	MUNICH	
CAIRO	NAGANO	

Solution on page 285

Laptop Computers

```
G G N I P Y T R A C K P A D
P W I R E L E S S D O M A E
S W Z X K I L S R P O O B L
R O T I N O M A U G B B I L
T R N I Z A O L M T E I H S
O K M Y R B A B H S T L S O
U P T G Y R T G R W O E O F
C Y O E F F I C I E N T T T
H R K R N L T F A I W R A W
P E D Q T R I H S P A O C A
A T C I J A E U I V M A P R
D T L K O O B T E N S O N E
M A C B O O K L N E E R C S
P B G N I M A G E I B O O K
```

BATTERY	KEYBOARD	NOTEBOOK	THIN
BUSINESS	LAP	POPULAR	TOSHIBA
CASE	LCD	PORTABLE	TOUCHPAD
COMPACT	LIGHT	POWERBOOK	TRACKPAD
DELL	MACBOOK	PROGRAMS	TRAVEL
EFFICIENT	MINI	SCREEN	TYPING
GAMING	MOBILE	SMALL	WIFI
IBOOK	MONITOR	SOFTWARE	WIRELESS
INTERNET	NETBOOK	SONY	WORK

Solution on page 285

Halloween Party

```
S C A C K L E R B A C A M E
N I G H T V M B L A C K E C
A C V E I A U T U M N R A N
C B O T H C T I W S I N O P
K S S B A N S H E E D O R U
S E P W W B O G E Y M A N N
F O I I K E C R W G N R G C
L M D C R I B O D K N O Q H
P U E K A M D S S L O A O Y
S S R E D A M S G D U R R K
E I S D H O G N I V R A C O
M C T S O H G E F O O D C O
A C Y R A C S T R E A T S P
G O B L I N N Y T R I C K S
```

AUTUMN	COSTUME	KIDS	SHADOWY
BANSHEE	DARK	MACABRE	SNACKS
BLACK	EERIE	MAKEUP	SPIDERS
BOGEYMAN	FESTIVE	MOON	SPOOKY
BROOMS	FOOD	MUSIC	TREATS
CACKLE	GAMES	NIGHT	TRICKS
CANDY	GHOST	ORANGE	WICKED
CARVING	GOBLIN	PRANKS	WITCH
CAULDRON	GOODIES	PUNCH	
COBWEBS	HORROR	SCARY	

Solution on page 286

174

Self-Help

```
E X E R C I S E B E L I E F
G Y C G O S R O I V A H E B
R O A N A P E G U I D E G O
O G G I C E W F C T D Z A O
W A N N H T O O E C I K I K
T P I R I S P C X A C N R L
H A Y A N T N U P O T O R A
Y T A E G E N S L R I W A N
P T R L U G V E O P O L M O
N E P L O A W A R E N E S S
O R F A M I L Y I A S D J R
S N L A N R E T N I P G P E
I S S E N T I F G M M E U P
S M O T I V A T E G U R U Y
```

ADDICTIONS
AWARENESS
BEHAVIORS
BELIEF
BOOK
COACHING
EXERCISE
EXPLORING
FAMILY
FITNESS

FOCUS
GOALS
GROWTH
GUIDE
GURU
HYPNOSIS
INFLUENCE
INTERNAL
KNOWLEDGE
LEARNING

MARRIAGE
MOTIVATE
PARENTING
PATTERNS
PERSONAL
POWER
PRAYING
PROACTIVE
STEPS
YOGA

Solution on page 286

Cool Things

```
P M E T A L T S O R F A V L
Z L S O D A P U U T W I M M
A M A R B L E F L O O R S K
P Y I Y A S E G D I R F M G
E N S S I U N S T R U G O Y
K I H D T N E M E S A B O S
A T N M G D G Z U E A E T W
L O I B N A E H P T H Q H I
P L G U I E S S O D U C I M
K A H R R E L O O C Z A E F
M S T B P F U C L R K W E D
W I N D S A S E G W B E N Z
A C S O Q N H A I R T E Y V
K E B T W S Y N D R A F T G
```

AIR	FEET	MIST	SORBET
AUTUMN	FRIDGE	NIGHT	SPLASH
BASEMENT	FROST	OCEAN	SPRING
BREEZE	FRUIT	PLAYING HOCKEY	SUNDAE
CHEESE	ICE	POND	SWIM
COOLER	IGLOO	POOL	TEA
DEW	LAKE	SLUSHY	WINDS
DRAFT	MARBLE FLOORS	SMOOTHIE	YOGURT
DRINK	METAL	SNOW	
FANS	MILK	SODA	

Solution on page 286

176

Tent

```
P Q K N I A R T N E T A R P
H I K I N G N I P M A C A U
S E Y U D N U O R G X B I T
E D F L B S R T P A R T Y E
P T A H B T E I C A N V A S
O R M M A M T U A I P H O R
R A I B O C E Q M U R U E O
K V L D H N P S P Y T B D O
C E Y I C Y U O S S C U A L
O L N O I L P M I A L G H F
V G T S R O O D T U O S S J
E S G Y C N E W E A T H E R
R E M M U S I Z E S H I P I
P O L E S E K A T S M A L L
```

ASSEMBLY	FABRIC	OUTSIDE	SETUP
BUGS	FAMILY	PARTY	SHADE
CAMPING	FLOOR	PEGS	SIZES
CAMPSITE	FUN	PITCHING	SMALL
CANVAS	GROUND	POLES	STAKES
CIRCUS	HIKING	POP UP	SUMMER
CLOTH	MOSQUITO	PORTABLE	TARP
COTS	NOMADS	PUP	TENT
COVER	NYLON	RAIN	TRAVEL
DOME	OUTDOORS	ROPES	WEATHER

Solution on page 286

In the Oven

```
M B K J F Z O F S Z H H T D
A I O O B W O O D U T C H C
S B O N K U Y N T I N Y H V
I D C C C O R T G H E A L H
M C B O I L I N G K M G I U
P A T R R M I Q R B E H O T
A K S O B Y A U E H L T R R
N E A O R F T R D A E R B A
L P O D N U M R E M I T A E
I I R L O R T N O C S H K S
K Z G H L N Y R A N G E E T
Q Z E H R A C K E E R A I O
Y A K I T C H E N I L X S P
T D I N N E R V F L M C O A
```

BAKE	CONTROL	GAS	PIES
BOILING	COOK	HEAT	PIZZA
BREAD	DINNER	HOT	POTS
BRICK	DOOR	KILN	RACK
BROIL	DRYING	KITCHEN	RANGE
BURN	DUTCH	KNOBS	ROAST
CAKE	ELEMENT	LIGHT	SEAR
CERAMIC	FIRE	MASONRY	TIMER
CHAMBER	FOOD	MITT	TURKEY
CLEAN	FURNACE	PAN	WOOD

Solution on page 287

Salty

```
Q R E K A H S P I H C C E Y
O C E A N Q K O O C K H L S
E R U S S E R P D O O L B W
T F N A T U R A L N S O A A
S L M R L A K E H D H R T T
A O X E L G U Y T I E I H E
T A D F N K J R L M R D X R
F T E I D G C D A E A E S A
A O R N U T R I E N T T U V
E U O E I M Y A H T T L Y A
C N H D T M S K I F E H S K
E T I H W T T H C N I P G S
Z E Y R O V A S R O S O U R
T E M G B F L A V O R U N D
```

BATH	DRY	NATURAL	SODIUM
BLOOD PRESSURE	FLAVOR	NUTRIENT	TABLE
BRINE	FLOAT	OCEAN	TASTE
CHIPS	FOOD	PINCH	WATER
CHLORIDE	GRAINS	REFINED	WHITE
CONDIMENT	HEALTH	RESTAURANT	
COOK	ION	ROCK	
CRYSTAL	KOSHER	SAVORY	
CURING	LAKE	SEA	
DIET	MINE	SHAKER	

Solution on page 287

IN Words

```
K X C I A C N E M X X I Y V
B D A B V M D I H W A B A A
H T C O Q Q N G H P H P I I
K L S G B E X C B T S K I N
U I Y T W V N B H C Y I N K
R W R O A I D I L M I N I U
Y S G A T S N I F I N D P P
K R U D I D B A S I N I R X
Q I U N M N E L H I I D A Y
M A G I I H I C O N A N I M
D I O A N N N J O N G I T E
N W P T E I G T N I H M N O
L N M I Z E N I V R N I Z K
D C T P D V R I N G N I K B
```

BASIN	GIN	KING	RUIN
BEING	GRIN	LINE	SING
BIN	HIND	MAIN	SKIN
BLIND	HINT	MIND	THIN
CHIN	INCH	MINE	TIN
COIN	INK	NINE	VAIN
FIND	INN	PAIN	VEIN
FINE	INTO	PIN	VINE
FINS	JOIN	RAIN	WIN
GAIN	KIND	RING	ZINC

Solution on page 287

Neighbors

```
H C T A W Q G R U M P Y B E
B L O U D N E L A C O L G C
I O S N E T I L O P E D O I
N S H E L P F U L Y S N S N
V E A W B A R B E C U E S C
I R R E N T E R S O O I I L
T O E D E Y S U K M H R P U
E W D S L E O I P M M F W D
I D Y I I I N T R U S I V E
U Y M T X D H M I N D F U L
Q A R O Y O E C V I S I T G
F A N U F G M N A T F I G N
P B K I D S T B T Y S O N I
O P E T S E T C E T O R P S
```

BARBECUES	GRUMPY	LOUD	PROTECT
CHILDREN	HELPFUL	MINDFUL	QUIET
CLOSE	HOUSE	NEW	RENTERS
COMMUNITY	INCLUDE	NICE	RESIDENT
COURTESY	INTRUSIVE	NOSY	ROWDY
DOGS	INVITE	OBNOXIOUS	RUDE
FAMILY	KIDS	PARTIES	SHARED
FRIENDLY	KIND	PETS	SINGLE
GIFT	LEND	POLITE	VISIT
GOSSIP	LOCAL	PRIVATE	WATCH

Solution on page 287

Farmers

```
R Y R T L U O P M C K X B Q
F W E M E R U T S A P X N X
H R R F G M U D L E I F L E
L A U A N I M A L S G J L S
F E N I V O B T R O U G H R
N I A M T K T H R E S H J U
C R M S F A L L O W T E S R
O K A G C E R I S W A L A A
W X R B M B N P M N O N O L
O H K O Z I O C S P G L H B
O A E U W R N O E E I O P I
L Y T A C B E E T S R T U B
E S K E T F H N D S D E E S
M D Q F L S Y I E L D R I Z
```

ANIMALS	FALLOW	MARKET	SEEDS
BARN	FARM	MILK	SHEEP
BEETS	FENCES	MUD	SILO
BIBS	FIELD	ORGANIC	SLOP
BOOTS	FRUIT	PASTURE	THRESH
BOVINE	GOATS	PIG	TROUGH
CATTLE	HAY	PLOW	WHEAT
COW	HORSE	POULTRY	WOOL
CROPS	JEANS	RANGE	WORK
DENIM	MANURE	RURAL	YIELD

Solution on page 288

Romance

```
S E L I M S T R A E H U G T
E L E V A R T R U O C S U G
V F R O S E S C I S U M N I
O E G O O W H H P D D E I F
D E N A M O R E D N E O T T
A L I E R L S R E O V P E S
T I N M A F E I U M O A D R
E N R O H W R S G A T S O A
T G A T C F E H I I I S T T
A S E I Y L N E R D O I I S
D S Y O D I A D T F N O N L
O I B N N R D A N C I N G O
R K A S O T E D I N I N G V
E C A R B M E S O P O R P E
```

ADORE	DIAMONDS	GIFTS	ROSES
BOND	DINING	HEARTS	SERENADE
BOYFRIEND	DOTING	HUG	SMILES
CANDLES	DOVES	INTRIGUE	STARS
CHARM	EMBRACE	KISS	TRAVEL
CHERISHED	EMOTIONS	LOVE	UNITED
COURT	ENAMORED	MUSIC	WOO
DANCING	FEELINGS	PASSION	YEARNING
DATE	FLIRT	POEMS	
DEVOTION	FLOWERS	PROPOSE	

Solution on page 288

Fried Food

```
D D E L I C I O U S C Y W E
A S E I R O L A C O I U O L
E E S E I R F Y R L R M N Z
R O A M P I D N L T A M T Z
B T U G O F D O C A M Y O I
U A S N W O R B H S A H N S
R T A I G G R Y E T L T S K
G O G N G T O H E Y A L H E
E P E E C I R R S R C A R W
R B A T T E R K E U Q E I E
S E O T A M O T R T M H M R
D J S A L L I T R O T N P N
H S I F S A L T E M P U R A
H E S A E R G J N O C A B P
```

BACON	DELICIOUS	OIL	TASTY
BATTER	DIP	PAN	TEMPURA
BREAD	EGG ROLL	PORK	TOMATOES
BURGERS	FATTENING	POTATOES	TORTILLAS
BUTTER	FISH	RICE	UNHEALTHY
CALAMARI	FRIES	SALT	WONTONS
CALORIES	GREASE	SAUSAGE	YUMMY
CHEESE	HASH BROWNS	SHRIMP	
CORN DOG	HOT	SIZZLE	
DEEP FRYER	MUSHROOMS	SKEWER	

Solution on page 288

Ancient History

```
R G N I N N I G E B S E G A
O M S Y M E S O L I T H I C C
C I R O T S I H E R P M O H
K P Y T N E I C N A A P T N
R T A G R I C U L T U R E S
E I F S O A H E O S A A Y T
C M R L T L O P T E N I T O
O E I O Y L O O G D C E I N
R P C O I S N E E E P G U E
D E A T E E O R A O D A Q H
E R H M A L T G C H R N I E
D I R G O H E H A E C O T N
C O E G A E Z N O R B R N G
J D Y L I N G U I S T I A E
```

AFRICA
AGES
AGRICULTURE
ANCIENT
ANTIQUITY
ARCHAEOLOGY
BEGINNING
BRONZE AGE
CULTURES
EARTH

EPOCH
ERA
GEOLOGY
ICE AGE
IRON AGE
LINGUIST
MESOLITHIC
MESOPOTAMIA
NEANDERTHAL
PALEOLITHIC

PAST
PREHISTORIC
RECORDED
ROCK RECORD
STONE AGE
STONEHENGE
TIME PERIOD
TOOLS

Solution on page 288

Surfing the Internet

```
S E M A G N E E R C S K D S
C I L I N K I F T A H C S O
E M A I L D P A I B B I E E
F A C E B O O K M R M L I D
N G U P H O E W O O E C B I
E E P S I Y M W N D D F B V
W S L C B C S I E L G O O G
S T O O R E T U P M O C H X
W O A N R O N U H C R A E S
O R D N R S S E R D D A D G
D I I E E R U S I E L T N O
N E N C U F O R U M S A U L
I S G T W I T T E R O D F B
W A L A P T O P T E L B A T
```

ADDRESS	E MAIL	LAPTOP	SHOP
BLOGS	FACEBOOK	LEISURE	STORIES
BROWSER	FIREFOX	LINK	TABLET
CHAT	FORUMS	LOADING	TWITTER
CLICK	FUN	MOBILE	UPLOAD
COMPUTER	GAMES	MONITOR	VIDEOS
CONNECT	GOOGLE	NEWS	WINDOWS
DATA	HOBBIES	PICTURES	
DOMAIN	IMAGES	SCREEN	
DOWNLOAD	KEYBOARD	SEARCH	

Solution on page 289

Sweet Tooth

```
Y F F A T P U D D I N G L A
A R F R U I T R U F F L E S
C O S B M B R O W N I E M O
E S A E U A E G D U F K A D
D T U L I B E I P C Y A R A
G I N G E R B R E A D H A P
S N A L A M T L C K N S C O
N G T E B R O S E E A K A P
I A B O N B O N A G C L V S
F D E S S E R T D P U I I I
F S W E E T E N E R O M T C
U O L A E R E C I R O C I L
M Q X J L O L L I P O P E E
P U R Y S P R I N K L E S O
```

BON BON	FROSTING	PASTRIES	SYRUP
BROWNIE	FRUIT	PIE	TAFFY
BUBBLEGUM	FUDGE	POPSICLE	TRUFFLE
CAKE	GINGERBREAD	PUDDING	
CANDY	ICE CREAM	ROOT BEER	
CARAMEL	LEMON DROPS	SODA POP	
CAVITIES	LICORICE	SORBET	
CEREAL	LOLLIPOP	SPRINKLES	
DECAY	MILK SHAKE	SUGAR	
DESSERT	MUFFINS	SWEETENER	

Solution on page 289

Wear Sunglasses

```
S E M A R F R E N G I S E D
P A E H C T H G I L N U S A
E A C C E S S O R Y V L L R
C D E Z I R A L O P O T O K
T N L L Z T D U R C E R O E
A I E C B E S O E C D A C N
C L B X T A T A A C I V O E
L B R N P E N F L Z S I L D
E V I T C E T O R P T O O R
S T T T A N N D I A U L R I
A V I A T O R S I H O E E V
W O E W Z V B D I O S T D I
N L S E S S A L G V R A C N
H C A E B R I G H T E B F G
```

ACCESSORY	DESIGNER	PLASTIC
AVIATORS	DIOR	POLARIZED
BEACH	DRIVING	PROTECTIVE
BLIND	EXPENSIVE	RADIATION
BRIGHT	FACE	SPECTACLES
CELEBRITIES	FASHIONABLE	SUNLIGHT
CHEAP	FRAMES	TAN
COLORED	GLASSES	TINTED
COOL	OCEAN	ULTRAVIOLET
DARKENED	OUTSIDE	UV PROTECTION

Solution on page 289

Survival Kit

```
D W A R M T H T L A E H F P
Z H S L O O T S N L F M L A
M E N N H L I A D M I I A O
T L N C O G I N S A N R R S
V P N I N I A G T P K R E L
W O D A C C T S H M I O D B
P A L H D I S A S T E R N L
R B T M S A D L R U E N I A
O F G E P A E E G P Y R T N
P P L M R U C A M P I N G K
E A O I C I U W H I S T L E
P C V S N Z F H A T C H E T
A K E M E T D O O F T N E T
T R S A F E T Y D B A G R P
```

ASPIRIN	FLINT	MEDICINE	SIGNAL
BAG	FOOD	MIRROR	SOAP
BLANKET	GAUZE	OINTMENT	TAPE
CAMPING	GLOVES	PACK	TARP
CANDLE	HATCHET	PONCHO	TENT
CASH	HEALTH	RADIO	TINDER
COMPASS	HELP	RATIONS	TOOLS
DISASTER	KNIFE	RESCUE	WARMTH
FIRE	LIGHTER	ROPE	WATER
FLARE	MAP	SAFETY	WHISTLE

Solution on page 289

Lecture

```
K L A T M U I D O P I T C H
L E A R N W A T E R E L A Y
C K A E P S C C H A A N D T
E G A U G N A L C N O L D O
N R E T C E L A C I T I R C
S R E C O R D S T A C S E G
T R E P X E E S P L U T S U
H E T Q M T E R S P R E S E
G B A I O U A O V X T N T S
I B C N Q T A O D E S K U T
L A U D T P I M L O N G D A
L J D L B V O C A L I Z E G
A M E O G N I L E S S O N E
H X X E N O R D I R E C T T
```

ACADEMIC
ADDRESS
CLASSROOM
CRITICAL
DESK
DIRECT
DRONE
EDUCATE
EXPERT
EXPLAIN

GUEST
HALL
INSTRUCT
JABBER
LANGUAGE
LEARN
LECTERN
LESSON
LIGHTS
LINGO

LISTEN
LONG
NOTES
ORAL
PITCH
PODIUM
PRATTLE
QUESTION
RECORD
RELAY

SOAPBOX
SPEAK
STAGE
STUDENT
TALK
VOCALIZE
WATER

Solution on page 290

Lighting Up the House

```
D I M M E D E S S E C E R R
L U M I N O S I T Y O G E E
S E L D N A C H N B L D I F
N E Y T N E C S E R O U L F
I C L F B R W I C I R G E I
A A T E O H O L S G S N D C
T L S P C B L L E H S I N I
R P O U L T G U D T E L A E
U E C U N N R M N E H I H N
C R B R I L L I A N C E C T
K I K Z S C O N C E R C T D
C F A L A M P A N I O Y I O
B L I N D S M T I T T A W O
B A O V E R H E A D A Y S M
```

BLAZING	CURTAINS	LUMINOSITY
BLINDS	DIMMED	MOOD
BRIGHTEN	EFFICIENT	OVERHEAD
BRILLIANCE	ELECTRICITY	PORCH
BULB	FIREPLACE	RECESSED
CANDLES	FLUORESCENT	SCONCE
CEILING	GLOW	SUN
CHANDELIER	ILLUMINATE	SWITCH
COLORS	INCANDESCENT	TORCHES
COSTLY	LAMP	WATT

Solution on page 290

Kites in the Sky

```
Y O O B M A B A B E A C H D
K T O Y I E I T H T A I L I
S P N W G R D E S I G N P A
T I A O C O D B R K J S O M
F R L R L D L S E X P S W O
I I A K K Y J O C O B G E N
L F G N I N N U R B R N R D
T E N H U A H T E O E I L T
G S I F T M K P A P E R I R
N E R D L I H C T H Z T N E
I N P G T C N L I G E S E E
Y I S E D R A G O N T U S M
L H S L I G H T N I N G L Z
F C I R B A F L O W O O D G
```

AERODYNAMIC	DESIGN	LIFT	SKY
AIRCRAFT	DIAMOND	LIGHTNING	SPORT KITES
ART	DRAGON	METEOROLOGY	SPRING
BAMBOO	FABRIC	NYLON	STRINGS
BEACH	FIGHTING	PAPER	TAIL
BIRDS	FLOW	PARK	TIE
BOX KITE	FLYING	POWER LINES	TOY
BREEZE	FUN	RECREATION	TREE
CHILDREN	GLUE	RUNNING	WING
CHINESE	HIGH	SILK	WOOD

Solution on page 290

Cheerleaders

```
P S P O R T H M E L I M S X
Y C S Y E L L A B T O O F D
P R G C I M C Y J U M P F A
P O O N H T A H T A L M C U
E W E T I O E G E L L O C Q
P D F V C T O T W E N P U S
R A I A V I I L C T R E S D
H T V M N A V C E H D V W D
Y H I G A S R S X E A E E U
T L F R K R T S R E N N A B
H E L J I I Y O I U C T T G
M T I A L P C P F T E S E N
R E P P R S S K V I Y X R O
C S S T L U A V S K I R T S
```

ACTIVITY	EXCITING	PEPPY	SPIRIT
ATHLETES	FANS	POM POM	SPLITS
BANNERS	FLIPS	PYRAMID	SPORT
CHANT	FOOTBALL	RALLY	SQUAD
CHEER	FUN	RHYTHM	SWEATER
COLLEGE	GAME	SCHOOL	TEAM
CONTEST	JUMP	SCORE	VARSITY
CROWD	KICK	SKIRT	VAULTS
DANCE	LOUD	SMILE	VICTORY
EVENTS	OUTGOING	SONG	YELL

Solution on page 290

Riding the Subway

```
R S E A T U N N E L I J U E
F A K T G N I T I A W I N D
A C I C R O D N E V I I E I
R X O L I R E T T I L T P R
E S S M S R O T A R E P O A
P R K A M I B V O R L L L C
P O D P P U G U C A U A E H
W O T N W O T N W O D T S J
O D S S E E O E S E E F H C
L X C T I C K E T N H O T E
E X P R E S S A J T C R O B
B U H Y O R S E H E S M O Q
T O K E N W S F D R A O B F
F A S T A N D N A B R U H Z
```

ARRIVAL	DOORS	LITTER	SEAT
BELOW	DOWNTOWN	MAP	SIGNS
BOARD	ENTER	OPERATOR	STAND
BOOTH	EXIT	PLATFORM	STOP
BRICKS	EXPRESS	POLES	TICKET
CAR	FARE	POSTERS	TOKEN
COMMUTE	FAST	RAILS	TUNNEL
CONCRETE	HUB	RIDE	URBAN
CROWD	KIOSK	ROUTE	VENDOR
DESCEND	LINE	SCHEDULE	WAITING

Solution on page 291

194

Cave Adventure

```
A C T I V I T Y G L O V E S
D L I W C R A W L I N G S S
E Q U I P M E N T T H G I L
G N S P E L U N K I N G C I
N G I E X Y D W I P S O R P
I S N M L G S E O B T P E P
B D U I N O I T S U A H X E
M I U O D L H E E C B R E R
I G R M R O A P G M E B A Y
L G F O L E O M E A L N R C
C I D I P L G L P E S E T S
O N N U F E Y N F S D S H N
L G T R O P S T A H D R A H
D L A C I S Y H P D K C A P
```

ACTIVITY	EARTH	LIGHT	SPELUNKING
BATS	EQUIPMENT	MINE	SPORT
CARABINER	EXERCISE	MUD	WET
CLIMBING	EXHAUSTION	PACK	WILD
COLD	FLOODING	PASSAGE	
CRAWLING	FUN	PHYSICAL	
DANGEROUS	GLOVES	POTHOLING	
DEEP HOLES	HARD HATS	ROPES	
DESCENT	HELMET	SLIPPERY	
DIGGING	LAMPS	SPELEOLOGY	

Solution on page 291

Dining Room

```
G U E S T S P I T C H E R S
K Z F P A A N I H C C O D E R
R T A O B Y V A R G L O S T
O S M O L Y N A P M O C R T
F G I N E D O L E F T R I I
L O L L E X I F H P H Y A N
O B Y L V G T L O P T S H G
W L I M H E A A L I N T C N
E E A T F N R T I C A A A I
R T I F H I O W D T G L B T
S N U W Z D C A A U E P I T
G B S A U C E R Y R L U N I
J S K N I R D E S E E C E S
G L A S S E S L I S N E T U
```

BUFFET	DECORATION	FORK	PITCHER
CABINET	DINE	GLASSES	SAUCER
CHAIRS	DRINKS	GOBLET	SETTING
CHANDELIER	EAT	GRAVY BOAT	SILVERWARE
CHINA	ELEGANT	GUESTS	SITTING
CLOTH	FAMILY	HOLIDAYS	SPOON
COMPANY	FLATWARE	HOST	TABLE
CRYSTAL	FLOWERS	LIGHTING	UTENSILS
CUP	FOOD	PICTURES	

Solution on page 291

Telecommunications

```
S E R V E R D C I N F O R M
Y K R E S C A N N I N G J O
S C E M C L T B U N A L P D
T O A L L E D N U O B N I E
E M C A R R I E R H B D C M
M P H N C O N V E Y N T T K
S U E G A M I C E A L W U R
H T D I W D N A B R I T R O
J E C S N A R D E R N C E W
L R I U T A A T E M E E S T
I J O S D O U L C R S N O E
A S I I R O E G O L A N A N
M D O B R S R E D I V O R P
E G A S S E M P V O I C E Z
```

ANALOG	E MAIL	NETWORK	ROUTER
BANDWIDTH	HUB	OUTBOUND	SCANNING
BROADBAND	IMAGE	PICTURES	SERVER
CALL	INBOUND	PLAN	SIGNAL
CARRIER	INFORM	PRODUCTS	SOUND
COMPUTER	INTERNET	PROVIDER	SYSTEMS
CONNECT	LINES	RADIO	VOICE
CONVEY	MESSAGE	REACH	WIRELESS
DISTANCE	MODEM	RECEIVER	

Solution on page 291

College Choices

```
B R I G H A M Y O U N G O C
P J X P Z N O T R E D A M E
Y U O C A R L E T O N N I R
H A R H I E B A Y L O R T O
T N L D N T T H L R B T W M
U O W E U S C E T C R L A H
O M F O N E H H K C A I K T
M O D N T W W O O U N B E R
T P E L O E E L P W D R F A
R P A R S S G M O K E E O W
A C I T I A M R O R I D R S
D A E T T C B E O R S N E G
O R W E L L E S L E Y A S L
N O T E C N I R P C G V T J
```

BAYLOR	DUKE	PURDUE
BRANDEIS	EMORY	RICE
BRIGHAM YOUNG	GEORGETOWN	SWARTHMORE
BROWN	JOHNS HOPKINS	USC
CALTECH	MIT	VANDERBILT
CARLETON	NORTHWESTERN	WAKE FOREST
CASE WESTERN	NOTRE DAME	WELLESLEY
CLEMSON	PENN STATE	YALE
COLGATE	POMONA	
DARTMOUTH	PRINCETON	

Solution on page 292

Historical

```
J G T S A P Y R A M I D S B
S N C K N O W L E D G E A N
T I M P O R T A N T M T R O
U D N N I S Y C G I T S E I
D L O O T E H I T L A E R T
Y I L I A R P S E S R T C C
R U Y G C U A S L H O T O I
T B B I O G R A P H Y A N F
S Q A L L I G L O K A N F A
E Q B E D F O C E O L C L M
C S D R O C E R P O T I I O
N O S T A L G I C B Y E C U
A M A R D M O N U M E N T S
Q C U L T U R E U Q I T N A
```

ANCESTRY	CLASSICAL	KNOWLEDGE	RELIGION
ANCIENT	CONFLICT	LOCATION	ROYALTY
ANTIQUE	CULTURE	MONUMENT	STUDY
ART	DRAMA	NOSTALGIC	TIMES
ATTESTED	ERA	OLD	
BABYLON	FAMOUS	PAST	
BATTLES	FICTION	PEOPLE	
BIOGRAPHY	FIGURES	PYRAMIDS	
BOOK	GEOGRAPHY	REAL	
BUILDING	IMPORTANT	RECORDS	

Solution on page 292

Auto Repair

```
S W I T C H Y W R E N C H H
T N I A P R E L F F U M S F
H E T N E R M E C H A N I C
G X K T A L I G N M E N T B
I H T S N U K C A J H L E R
L A O N A A T A R I E X G A
B U O O O G C O B B T A H K
O S L E D I I I M E R U C E
D T S T A R T E R A R I L S
Y O I L E O U I G B T I U A
H U B T R Q O E N S U I T E
Y T N A R R A W P G H L C R
X I F O E N G I N E I O H G
M O T O R A D I A T O R P D
```

ALIGNMENT	EXTERIOR	INTERIOR	SHOP
AUTOMATIC	FIX	JACK	STARTER
BATTERY	GARAGE	LIGHTS	SWITCH
BELT	GASKET	LUBRICANT	TIRE
BODY	GREASE	MECHANIC	TOOLS
BRAKES	HOOD	MOTOR	TORQUE
CLUTCH	HOSE	MUFFLER	WARRANTY
DIPSTICK	HUB	OIL	WRENCH
ENGINE	IGNITION	PAINT	
EXHAUST	INHIBITOR	RADIATOR	

Solution on page 292

Hobby

```
E T Y R L E W E J C H E S S
T P E T S E R E T N I P E K
A E G N I U Q I T N A A L O
E E M W N V E F L I G G Z O
R R K I E I I S N O N G Z B
C T E I T S S T Y B I N U R
R Y F L H S I A C E T I P I
A U C I A N A M G A L P T D
F E N L G X T P N D I M R G
T G K N I T I S I W U A A E
R E A D I N G N G O Q C V C
W R I T I N G U G R W O E N
T B A K I N G F O K G O L A
S L E D O M Y O J N E K T D
```

ACTIVITY	COOK	JEWELRY	RELAXING
ANTIQUING	CRAFT	JOGGING	RUNNING
ART	CREATE	KNIT	SEW
BAKING	CYCLING	MODELS	STAMPS
BEADWORK	DANCE	PAINTING	TENNIS
BOOKS	ENJOY	PASTIME	TRAVEL
BRIDGE	FISHING	PETS	WRITING
BUILDING	FUN	PUZZLES	YOGA
CAMPING	HIKE	QUILTING	
CHESS	INTEREST	READING	

Solution on page 292

In the Attic

```
L I S E H T O L C H E S T B
A N U H I S T O R Y V E O U
D S I S L L A B H T O M Y G
D E T E M C R A F T E R S S
E C C R D O A N T I Q U E S
R T A U G S O R D F K X S B
E S S T H K N L D K O Q M E
C T E I O N W O R B U L A W
O N I N S U L A T I O N E B
R E R R T J D S R E E A B O
D M O U S E T R A P L H R C
S R M F D N E R E S S E R D
T A E H E L U G G A G E K G
B G M V S E R U S A E R T S
```

ANTIQUES	DUST	LADDER	SUITCASE
BEAMS	FURNITURE	LOFT	TOYS
BOXES	GARMENTS	LUGGAGE	TREASURES
BUGS	GHOSTS	MEMORIES	VENTS
CARDBOARD	HEAT	MOTHBALLS	
CHEST	HEIRLOOMS	MOUSETRAP	
CLOTHES	HISTORY	RAFTERS	
COBWEBS	INSECTS	RECORDS	
DARK	INSULATION	SKELETONS	
DRESSER	JUNK	SQUIRRELS	

Solution on page 293

Mother

```
S M O M K S E L F L E S S I
U T S R E G R N G G U N L F
P N E E E N F E A U U X A W
P E I D S I D R T G I M N E
O R R N U R U D G H I D R S
R A O E N O B L E L G A E S
T P T T C D E I Y T C U T I
E N S N A A U H A N O R A K
G H E P O E R C O E O V M D
A E C I E S R R L N M S E U
M L N O T C P C G E B O O D
A P A T O A I Y T E A C H N
M E V O L K P A O M B N U I
U R S W E E T Y L J Y F G K
```

ADORING	DEVOTED	KIND	SELFLESS
ANCESTOR	ENCOURAGE	KISS	SNUGGLE
APRON	FAMILY	LOVE	SON
BABY	FUN	MAMA	SPECIAL
CARE	GENTLE	MATERNAL	STORIES
CHILDREN	GUIDE	MEND	STRONG
CLEAN	HELPER	MOM	SUPPORT
COOK	HOME	NOBLE	SWEET
CREATOR	HUG	PARENT	TEACH
DAUGHTER	JOY	PATIENT	TENDER

Solution on page 293

Tiny Things

```
L T P R O T O Z O A S X D C
I R A Y S T E B N P N E A W
A I E D B G I L M E E T E Q
N N P M P A G U P S T R B U
E K B I R O B E Q O H T U A
E E U C N E L B H S R A I R
D T T R S P G E B S O D A K
L A T O A X A R E T I M E G
E N O B B T H R E A D F L N
C G N E E N O I T C A R F I
I S N R O B W E N I A R G L
R A T O M D U S T O C K E P
C E L L A G U B Y D A L N A
T E L E Y E G M A R B L E S
```

AMOEBA	EYELET	LADYBUG	PIN
ANT	FISH EGGS	MARBLES	PROTOZOA
ATOM	FLEA	MICROBE	QUARK
BABY	FRACTION	MITE	RICE
BEAD	GENE	MOSQUITO	SAPLING
BLUEBERRIES	GERM	NAIL	SEED
BUTTON	GNAT	NEEDLE	SHREW
CELL	GOOSE BUMPS	NEWBORNS	TADPOLE
DROPLET	GRAIN	PARTICLE	THREAD
DUST	KITTEN	PEA	TRINKET

Solution on page 293

Front Porch

```
S T H G I L H E Y P O N A C
E V H O C O D F A E L B A T
A A C R U O R I W F M D E I
T C N S O I V G H E N S H S
I C E W E C N E C A S T W I
N E B N E I K N R T A O E V
G S D O T I A E A E D O M Y
N S C I O R V M R N D L O N
I P V O T K Y W I P O T C O
L N L N F L O W E R S D L C
I Z E A V F E D A N O M E L
A W N I N G E A E Y Q O W A
R I A H C T N E E R C S D B
X T E S N U S T A I R S W X
```

ACCESS	DOOR	PLANTS	TEA
ARCHWAY	ENTRANCE	POT	VERANDA
AWNING	ENTRYWAY	RAILING	VIEW
BALCONY	FLOWERS	ROCKER	VISIT
BENCH	FRIENDS	SCREEN	WELCOME
BOOK	HOUSE	SEATING	WINDOWS
CANOPY	INVITING	STAIRS	WOOD
CHAIR	LEMONADE	STOOL	WREATH
COFFEE	LIGHTS	SUNSET	
COVERED	MATS	TABLE	

Solution on page 293

Optometrist

```
S M E D I C A L A I P O Y M
I K T D I S O R D E R S R E
C C O R N E A V R Q C I E T
L O O R E G N I F U A O S A
E S R Y S A P E M I T C A L
A I E R S H T W A P A U L I
R G G C E I C M X M R L A D
E H L R N C S O E E A A C I
R T A B D A T O N N C R O S
O L U L N R R I N T T T F E
T A C U I T Y U V G A Y I A
C E O R L E N S S E A C R S
O H M R B R E T I N A I T E
D N A Y S L A C O F I B D S
```

ACUITY	DIAGNOSIS	FINGER	OCULAR
BIFOCALS	DILATE	GLAUCOMA	PERIPHERAL
BLINDNESS	DISEASES	HEALTH	RETINA
BLURRY	DISORDERS	INSURANCE	SIGHT
CATARACT	DOCTOR	IRIS	TREATMENT
CLEARER	DRY	LASER	TRIFOCAL
CONTACTS	EQUIPMENT	LENS	VIEW
CORNEA	EXAM	MEDICAL	
CORRECTIVE	EYE	MYOPIA	

Solution on page 294

Fun at the Fair

```
Y I C E C R E A M K D K Z V
A D N O V E L T I E S C G K
W S N O I T I T E P M O C W
D T H A B N G A M E S T O L
I F S G C B T B D K T S N A
M A E R P N I O Y O H E C V
S R N I R U O R S T G V E I
N C O C I F I T E S I I S N
O I C U Z D Y K T U L L S R
O D W L E J S N W O L C I A
L N O T S E T N O C C B O C
L A N U R I D E P A S S N E
A H S R A C R E P M U B S S
B A K E D G O O D S W O H S
```

AGRICULTURE	CONCESSIONS	LIVESTOCK
BAKED GOODS	CONTEST	MIDWAY
BALLOONS	COTTON CANDY	NOVELTIES
BLUE RIBBON	FOOD	PRIZES
BUMPER CARS	FUN	RACES
CARNIVAL	GAMES	RIDE PASS
CLOWNS	HANDICRAFTS	SHOWS
COIN TOSS	ICE CREAM	SKY RIDE
COMPETITIONS	LIGHTS	SNOW CONES

Solution on page 294

Measuring

```
S H S L E H S U B P U C H J
S N S G U L S E U G A E L P
M N O U N C E S K W C L H O
K N O T S O T I M T E S C I
N I V L E K L E A D E I A N
A W K I L O G R A M S U M T
W Z C I W A E R U S C S I S
Q A T A W S G C M F P J C E
S E T A L I L O I A I O R H
R T T T T O H E R R N U O C
S T A N H T R S R U T L N N
S G E R A O E I P R S E S I
R C R F A C U E E I A S M O
D Y N E S C F R F S K B E C
```

BARRELS	FATHOMS	KIPS	PINTS
BUSHELS	FEET	KNOTS	POINTS
CALORIES	FURLONGS	LEAGUES	SLUGS
CARATS	GALLONS	LITER	TEASPOON
CELSIUS	HECTARES	MACH	TONS
CENTIGRADE	INCHES	MEGAWATTS	WATT HOUR
CUP	JOULES	METRIC	
DYNES	KELVIN	MICRONS	
EMS	KILOGRAMS	OUNCES	
ERGS	KILOWATTS	PARSECS	

Solution on page 294

Jokes

```
N H U M O R K N A R P L Y J
S W G I G G L E G A G K R E
T C I T N A V C R E U C O S
Y L S T E Q U O C U E L T T
L U H A T N D D R V T A S W
L B O Y R Y I F I P G S F E
I K R D N C T T W E M S E H
S P T E P N A R U Q N I A G
A U J M W E U S I O U C R U
T N C O R T S F M D R I E A
I W C C K T I M I N G R P L
R O C O M I C S B L H O A L
E L D D I R N A E L C N C E
K C I R T W R G O O F Y D T
```

ANTIC	CREATIVE	JEST	SATIRE
AUDIENCE	DIRTY	JOKING	SHORT
BAR	FUNNY	LAUGH	SILLY
CAPER	GAG	PARODY	STAGE
CLASSIC	GESTURE	PRANK	STORY
CLEAN	GIGGLE	PUN	TELL
CLOWN	GOOFY	QUIP	TIMING
CLUB	HUMOR	RIDDLE	TRICK
COMEDY	IMPROV	ROUTINE	WITTY
COMICS	IRONY	SARCASM	WRITTEN

Solution on page 294

Creative Writing

```
O B N V J W M A G A Z I N E
Z D I A L O G U E P R O S E
C T H O U G H T S D I J N C
L N A F G E E M O T I O N R
A E I A K R L A N G U A G E
S L K C O U A E G N U N L A
S A U T O T V P S T I B Z T
E T M U B N V M H L A H Y I
T L O A I E T O E Y H S X V
T E N L R V R E O O A I A E
I V T B P D F J S T P L M R
N O S Q R A N O N T P B I N
G N I D A E R A F E S U L E
N O I T C I F T N I R P C G
```

ADVENTURE	DRAMA	IDEA	PRINT
AUTHOR	EMOTION	INVENTION	PROSE
BIOGRAPHY	ENJOYABLE	LANGUAGE	PUBLISH
BOOK	FACTUAL	MAGAZINE	READING
CLASS	FANTASY	NOUNS	SETTING
CLIMAX	FEELING	NOVEL	SONG
CONTESTS	FICTION	PEN	TALENT
CREATIVE	GENRE	PLOT	THOUGHTS
DIALOGUE	HAIKU	POEM	VERBS

Solution on page 295

Slow Things

```
E F O T U R T L E D E L A Y
W A L K I N G N I C N A D S
O C G O M J H T W O R G R E
R R N N G O T L I E N R I A
K E O E I A L T W I O E P S
D E I I D H U A H A X B S O
A P S P N L C T S F R E E N
Y T O I O C A T I S R C I S
D L R V O E H S E G E I B E
E E E A R T H W O R M S M K
T B C B F I R R O Y T I O I
O O G A N F P O O R T S Z H
U I W G Y K I G T B M H U W
R L Z E O N A C E Z E E R B
```

BOIL	DELAY	HIKES	TIME
BREATHING	DETOUR	ICEBERG	TORTOISE
BREEZE	DRIP	INCHWORM	TRAFFIC
BUS	EARTHWORMS	MOLASSES	TURTLE
CANOE	EROSION	PROGRESS	WALKING
CRAWL	EVOLUTION	ROAST	WORKDAY
CREEP	FISHING	SEASONS	YOGA
DANCING	GOLF	STRETCHING	ZOMBIES
DECAY	GROWTH	TADPOLE	

Solution on page 295

Music Lessons

```
S G N O S L V P I T C H I R
P L O Y T I L I B A I P R A
T E M P O D T I R X S R O T
Y A L L N E D P K R U I T E
L R I R E T E M O S M V U S
K N O H K G C T E P X A T E
E T S E G N N L R G J T E L
E M G I H E A O U U L E A A
W H O N M T V N T I M Z C C
S T B Z I E D A S D F P H S
T Y O C T G A I O E L O E W
A H E U U O N P P A R T R T
N R L A C O V I Y D O L E M
D F T N E D U T S N C O D A
```

ABILITY	MELODY	PRIVATE	STUDENT
ADVANCED	MENTOR	RATES	TEACH
ARPEGGIO	METER	RECITAL	TEMPO
CHORDS	MUSIC	RHYTHM	THEORY
CODA	NOTES	SCALES	TONE
FLUTE	OBOE	SHEET	TRUMPET
FORM	PIANO	SINGING	TUTOR
GUIDE	PITCH	SKILL	VIOLIN
IMPROVE	PLAY	SONGS	VOCAL
LEARN	POSTURE	STAND	WEEKLY

Solution on page 295

Teaching

```
M K P R A C T I C E H Z Y S
Y S C H O O L S Z O I A R U
G E R F M E L I M U S O S B
N D E A C L R E Q S T N O J
I Q T T E O W D E U O X E E
D H U B M O M U T I R K G C
A R P E R U H C T S Y D A T
E G M K S C H A L K E U U S
R N O I C T U T N L M T G I
A I C E I Q I I W D R I N S
S T U D E N T O B O O K A S
E I R I N B N N N Y F U L A
R R T U C K R E W S N A T R
N W P G E L P O F F I C E T
```

ANSWER	ERASER	LECTURE	SCHOOL
ART	ESSAY	MATH	SCIENCE
ASSIST	GUIDE	MEMORIZE	STUDENT
BELLS	GYM	MUSIC	SUBJECTS
BOOK	HANDOUT	OFFICE	TEST
CHALK	HISTORY	PEN	TUTOR
COMPUTER	HOMEWORK	PRACTICE	WRITING
DESK	INFORM	QUESTIONS	
EDUCATION	KNOWLEDGE	QUIZ	
EQUATIONS	LANGUAGE	READING	

Solution on page 295

All Kinds of Floors

```
D U R A B L E P E Z C E C T
T N E M E C A T T L L R O R
U G M U A R A I E B C K L I
O Q L F Q N H A R D W O O D
R L R U I G N A C E A Z R D
G U E M E I M O N K T Z E K
S T A I N S V O O B M A B D
L L P G V E U C C U S R M R
I Y G A R D R B E O S R U U
A G N I T A O L F R D E L B
N S N I T T O T S L A T E B
L G L R V N E X T H O M E E
Q E O V I C A R P E T O I R
S M C L A Y F I N I S H R C
```

BAMBOO	DIRT	MARBLE	SUBFLOOR
CARPET	DURABLE	MATERIAL	SURFACE
CEMENT	FINISH	MORTAR	TERRAZZO
CERAMIC	FLOATING	NAILS	TILES
CLAY	GLUE	OAK	VINYL
CLEANING	GROUT	PARQUET	
COLOR	HARDWOOD	PATTERN	
CONCRETE	HOME	RUBBER	
CORK	LAMINATE	SLATE	
COVERING	LINOLEUM	SOFT	
DESIGN	LUMBER	STAIN	

Solution on page 296

Fancy Handwriting

```
D O C U M E N T S Y O B W F
C H I N E S E P E H H I O O
H S U R B K N I C P P N R N
C P D R A H A R I A A U D T
D H I E O M I C T R R E S S
B R A H L M S S C G C V H L
W E L R S I A U A O H I S A
B P A H A N C N R P M S I N
L A I U C C A A P Y E S R G
A P C I T R T M T T N E U U
C R E A T I V E N E T R O A
K N P I V Q F I R E S P L G
T S S E M A N U J S P X F E
K T T E B A H P L A T E X T
```

ALPHABET	DOCUMENTS	PARCHMENT
ANCIENT	EXPRESSIVE	PENMANSHIP
ARTIST	FLOURISH	PRACTICE
ASIAN	FONTS	ROMAN
BEAUTIFUL	HARD	SERIF
BLACK	INK BRUSH	SPECIAL
CHARACTERS	LANGUAGE	TEXT
CHINESE	MANUSCRIPT	TYPOGRAPHY
CREATIVE	NAMES	WORDS
DECORATIVE	NIB	
DELICATE	PAPER	

Solution on page 296

Department Stores

```
V A R I E T Y U E S E A R S
Y S H O E S P S L A R N E S
M A L L S S N R P D E C G H
S H W F C R I P S M I B I I
Y A A A U G A T M O H A S P
U P L T Y R N A H G S T T P
D E E E E A N C N N A H R I
I R I L F N L I H S C O Y N
S S T N E O N P T G D S R G
C E I Q T E U E S U D T L L
O Z U H D R F Y C I R L E O
U I E R S U O T K A D E W V
N S A E L B S E I B A B E E
T G N I D D E B T O Y S J S
```

APPAREL	FURNITURE	MEN	TIE
BABIES	GARDENING	PRODUCTS	TOYS
BATH	GIRLS	PURSE	UPSCALE
BEDDING	GLOVES	REGISTRY	VARIETY
BELTS	HAT	RETURNS	
BOYS	INFANTS	SALE	
CASHIER	JEWELRY	SEARS	
CHOICES	KIDS	SHIPPING	
CLOTHES	LAYAWAY	SHOES	
DISCOUNT	MALLS	SIZES	
DISPLAY	MANNEQUIN	TASTEFUL	

Solution on page 296

Fancy Restaurant

```
H E V I S U L C X E V O D F
Y N P Y T I L A U Q F A E I
A G J N C O U R S E S H S N
T A M B I A N C E C C T S E
T P T J H K C U I S I N E C
I M O M T A P I T L F E R N
R A K R O F D A L A S L T A
E H O C L S O U N E M U S G
C C D R C B P C L M D P O E
I I E O E W Y H K T V O C L
V R X C L E X P E N S I V E
R T U E B S U O I R U X U L
E A T D A R E Z I T E P P A
S C U L T U R E D I N I N G
```

ADULTS	DECOR	MENU
AMBIANCE	DELICACY	NAPKIN
APPETIZER	DESSERT	OPULENT
ATMOSPHERE	DINING	QUALITY
ATTIRE	ELEGANCE	RICH
CHAMPAGNE	EXCLUSIVE	SALAD FORK
CHEF	EXPENSIVE	SAUCEBOAT
COST	FANCY	SERVICE
COURSES	FINE	TABLECLOTH
CUISINE	LUXURIOUS	TUXEDO
CULTURED	MEALS	VASE

Solution on page 296

Bedroom

```
C W O D N I W B D F U T O N
B O O K S T E E H S U R B R
P L V G C Y C A V I R P H Q
M L A E O O W L Y T I N A V
B I T N R E T R O F M O C C
L P R A K S C H E S T G U R
I S T R B E R E S S E R D P
N E S D O L T V M X T T H O
D P O E A R E D R A W E R S
S A T S R E P P I L S M M T
L R O O D T R N S E R E N E
E D H O R E T E P R A C H R
E E P M A L S A M A J A P S
P B C H A I R K M A S T E R
```

BED	CORKBOARD	LAMP	RELAX
BLANKET	COVERS	MASTER	SERENE
BLINDS	CURTAIN	MATTRESS	SHEETS
BOOK	DECORATED	MIRROR	SLEEP
BRUSH	DESK	PAJAMAS	SLIPPERS
CARPET	DOOR	PHOTOS	TABLE
CHAIR	DRAPES	PILLOW	VANITY
CHEST	DRAWERS	POSTERS	WINDOW
CLOSET	DRESSER	PRIVACY	
COMFORTER	FUTON	READ	

Solution on page 297

Small Business

```
S P L T D E M P L O Y E E A
T U E I I N D I V I D U A L
O R N D O T M A N A G E D A
R S D E Y E D K M C C B V T
E U E R T R A I A C O O I I
T I R C L P E O R O L P S P
A T S U A R H S K U L E O A
V E T L I I R K E N A R R C
I G C T C S E E T T T A E O
R D U U E E V M N A E T E M
P U D R P P O H S N R E R P
M B O E S A U D I T A W A A
P F R A N C H I S E L L C N
Y R P G N I L L A C O L P Y
```

ACCOUNTANT	CREDIT	MARKET
ADVISOR	CULTURE	OPERATE
AUDIT	EMPLOYEE	OVERHEAD
BOOKKEEPER	ENTERPRISE	PLANNER
BUDGET	FRANCHISE	PRIVATE
CALLING	INDIVIDUAL	PRODUCTS
CAPITAL	KIOSK	PURSUIT
CAREER	LENDERS	SHOP
COLLATERAL	LOCAL	SPECIALTY
COMPANY	MANAGE	STORE

Solution on page 297

Dairy Products

```
C D E R U T L U C L K P P T
U H E D W H E Y O G U R T S
R D E Z I N E G O M O H E K
D R I E I I P E S C Z K I L
S G A U S R A R E N A G R I
N D A D Q E U S O H L D B M
T P L T D I S E S T L S A D
B U U O E E L L T P E E H S
D D M T D F H A L S R I B K
W D R A T S U C C C A R N I
B I O L R E T T U B Z P T M
F N F E Y E L O H W Z A V H
E G S G G E E S S U O M W H
R N U D R I F E K G M C Y S
```

BRIE	FORMULA	PROCESSED
BUTTER	GELATO	PROTEIN
CHEDDAR	GOAT	PUDDING
CHEESE	HOMOGENIZED	SHAKES
COW	KEFIR	SHEEP
CREAM	LACTOSE	SKIM
CULTURED	LIQUID	WHEY
CURDS	MILK	WHOLE
CUSTARD	MOUSSE	YOGURT
EGGS	MOZZARELLA	
FETA	PASTEURIZED	

Solution on page 297

Researching

```
S E A R C H N O I T A T I C
P R O C E S S E L C I T R A
U R B E I V Y I A B S E E T
B A O D R R I D S O J N L A
L O E J A O E E L E P R G D
I A O M E M L V W R H E O S
S I I K I C E P O M Y T O Y
H R L C H D T B X C M N G R
P E A A N A L Y Z E S I N A
A S C T N E T N A R G I I R
P U I E M R R S T U D Y D B
E L D S R A U Y R I U Q N I
R T E T E R D O H T E M U L
S S M L E K Y O J T C A F L
```

ACADEMIC	GRANT	PAPERS	STUDY
ANALYZE	IDEAS	PRIMARY	TEST
ARTICLES	INQUIRY	PROBLEMS	THESIS
BOOK	INTERNET	PROCESS	
CITATION	JOURNAL	PROJECT	
DATA	LAB	PUBLISH	
DISCOVER	LEARN	READ	
EXPLORE	LIBRARY	RESULTS	
FACT	MEASURE	REVIEW	
FUNDING	MEDICAL	SEARCH	
GOOGLE	METHOD	SOLVE	

Solution on page 297

Great Words

```
T E R R I F I C R E T T E B
S G L S O L I D P T S R I F
E N T B P R E E M I N E N T
R I K A A B E S T X R C S S
A H T A E R G S F E D H U O
E S O M L N A A S P E A P M
D A P E I D V P A L L M E E
O M S D A O E R M O L P R R
O S A B R C A U T O E I L O
G E T A T M D S O C C O A F
L O B A O A K N H A X N T E
N L B U N E Q U A L E D I I
E L N D E L A V I R N U V H
E T Y N R O I R E P U S E C
```

BEST	GREAT	SMASHING
BETTER	HOT	SOLID
CHAMPION	INCOMPARABLE	SUPERIOR
CHIEF	KEEN	SUPERLATIVE
COOL	LEADING	TERRIFIC
DANDY	NEAT	TOPS
DEAREST	NOT BAD	UNEQUALED
FAVORABLE	PARAMOUNT	UNEXCELLED
FIRST	PEERLESS	UNRIVALED
FOREMOST	PREEMINENT	UNSURPASSED
GOOD	RESPECTABLE	

Solution on page 298

Fitness Club

```
S H M A C H I N E S Y M C A
V S G N M Y T I L I C A F A
T H E A L T H L X M R E E T
S S E N L L E W E D L R R N
G T E C T B R M I L O M O E
S R F E B I B O I B V U W M
B E O M F E F P I A W I I P
S A U U R O T C U R T S N I
T D R S P I S E K I B A G U
R M H B C S W I M M I N G Q
O I E A E L C S U M L M B E
P L L G C L A S S E S Y I O
S L O O P I L A T E S G O B
O S C Y C L E S I C R E X E
```

AEROBICS	FEES	ROWING
BARBELLS	FITNESS	SPORTS
BIKES	GROUP	STEAM
CARDIO	GYMNASIUM	SWIMMING
CLASSES	HEALTH	TREADMILLS
CYCLE	INSTRUCTOR	WELLNESS
DUMBBELLS	MACHINES	YMCA
ELLIPTICAL	MEMBERSHIP	YOGA
EQUIPMENT	MUSCLE	
EXERCISE	PILATES	
FACILITY	POOLS	

Solution on page 298

Faces

```
T L A F A C H F X O V A L F
E P O G H P Y P M U R G R S
S L E E P Y R A C S L O H P
P D E L A T E D E A W S J I
U K M M O U T H S N C O R L
S R E K O P F S R A E R C I
X E X C I T E D E V D R I N
D R H D C S I R D H Y O E E
G A U N T K E O A I S W H S
E U T U N F U N N Y D A I L
L Q I O I G S G G E P L L H
I S R R H N N E R P L U M P
M E E Y C E I O Y Y O U N G
S X D A M P B Z L E S O N E
```

AGED	EYES	MAD	SLEEPY
ANGRY	FROWN	MOUTH	SMILE
BORED	FUNNY	NOSE	SORROW
CHEEKS	GAUNT	OVAL	SQUARE
CHIN	GLASSES	PLUMP	TIRED
CRYING	GRUMPY	POKER	UPSET
DOUGHY	HAPPY	ROUND	YOUNG
EARS	LASHES	SAD	
ELATED	LINES	SCARY	
EMOTION	LIPS	SERENE	
EXCITED	LONG	SILLY	

Solution on page 298

Running Errands

```
S V Y P O H S G N I T E E M
T N E M T N I O P P A G S P
O T J T G N I V I R D N B U
R A G X E S Y R T P A I D K
E S R S R R T A U C G R V C
S K O U L A I R K A D U D I
C H C N U L C N S P E E R P
H X E Q O H I S A A N F E H
E G R R A B T B Q R T F T A
D L I S T A S R U K I U U R
U L E F T N E O I I S A R M
L A S I T K M U C N T H N A
E M O D P S O T K G F C S C
T N U A J E D E L I V E R Y
```

APPOINTMENT	GAS STATION	PURCHASE
BANK	GIFTS	QUICK
BILLS	GROCERIES	ROUTE
CAR	JAUNT	SCHEDULE
CHAUFFEURING	LIST	SHOP
DELIVERY	LUNCH	SNACK
DENTIST	MALL	STORE
DOMESTICITY	MEETINGS	TAILOR
DRIVING	PARKING	TASK
DVD RETURNS	PHARMACY	TRIP
EXCURSION	PICK UP	VETERINARIAN

Solution on page 298

Wealthy

```
Q H S I V A L D E T H C A Y
T T L U A V E T A T S E S T
R E N W O D B O A T S D T N
A R N G A M M O E A N G O E
V I E O L C A S F O R I C L
E T L L Z H S F B E S N K P
L E R D T A L L E N A T S Y
S R E A B U N D A N C E R T
E L N U E F B M I T V J E I
N U U N Z F C F J A I Y Y R
A X T T S E V N I B M P W A
L U R R M U N I T A L P A H
P R O P E R T Y E N O M L C
P Y F U N D S A D K S R A C
```

ABUNDANCE	CHAUFFEUR	JET	PLATINUM
AFFLUENT	ENVY	LAVISH	PLENTY
ASSETS	ESTATE	LAWYERS	PROPERTY
BANK	FAMOUS	LOADED	RETIRE
BOATS	FINANCE	LUXURY	STOCKS
BONDS	FORTUNE	MAID	TRAVEL
BUTLER	FUNDS	MANSION	VAULT
CAPITAL	GOLD	MONEY	YACHT
CARS	GREED	OWNER	
CHARITY	INVEST	PLANES	

Solution on page 299

Fragrance

```
B I T W O I L S B T H C E T
S R E W O L F G G A I C N S
E C E N E T E N E T K A I P
E O W M I C I A R M T E P R
L F S D L M N U T U T M R A
P F C O L A S E R H R U O Y
M E V A I R U A E F E F N R
A E C L N Q L N J C E R O O
S W F C U D G O D S I E S V
A S R O D O L E N R M P E A
C C B H L H S E R F Y U S S
H E X O T I C E S T E R S Y
E N C L N N R O C P O P X K
T T T A I A M O R A P A O S
```

AIR	COFFEE	LEATHER	RICH
ALCOHOL	COLOGNE	MUSK	SACHET
ANISE	ESTERS	NATURAL	SAMPLE
AROMA	EXOTIC	NOSE	SAVORY
BAKERY	FLOWER	NUTMEG	SCENT
BOUQUET	FRESH	ODOR	SMELL
CALMING	FRUIT	OILS	SOAP
CANDLES	INCENSE	PERFUME	SPICE
CITRUS	JASMINE	PINE	SPRAY
CLOVES	LAUNDRY	POPCORN	SWEET

Solution on page 299

Recycle Things

```
G N I G A K C A P L A N E T
B E C O L O G Y G R E N E W
A W N G A R B A G E A R T H
L S O N X S E C R U O S E R
U P I S O E A G A H C L D G
M A T E R I A L S N L R R S
I P U L S R T A V I S E A C
N E L T S E R C F A N T O I
U R L T A T L D E I G N B T
M N O O L T N I A L S E D S
G Z P B G A H T T U L C R A
S T E E L B N X M X H O A L
T S O P M O C E S U E R C P
E L C Y C E R Z S L A T E M
```

ALUMINUM	CONSUMER	LANDFILL	RECYCLE
BATTERIES	CONTAINER	MATERIALS	RENEW
BOTTLES	EARTH	METALS	RESOURCES
CANS	ECOLOGY	NEWSPAPER	REUSE
CARDBOARD	ENERGY	PACKAGING	SALVAGE
CENTER	GARBAGE	PLANET	STEEL
COLLECTION	GLASS	PLASTICS	TEXTILES
COMPOST	GREEN	POLLUTION	TRASH

Solution on page 299

Presidents' Day

```
N A T I O N S H O P P I N G
V N S X M O N D A Y T P O N
A L A K C E L E B R A T E I
C O M M E M O R A T I O N D
A C I R E M A D R N H H O N
T N F L A G I I Z U B F T U
I I H I S T O R Y O U E G O
O L A V I T S E F C N B N F
N A R O I Z Y A D H T R I B
R R N S E G A M I D I U H E
M E M O R I A L U E N A S L
E D I R P Y S N I A G R A B
F E I H C H O L I D A Y W O
V F L O A T S L E A D E R N
```

AMERICA	DEAD	HOLIDAY	PATRIOTISM
BARGAINS	FEBRUARY	IMAGES	PRIDE
BIRTHDAY	FEDERAL	LEADER	SHOPPING
BUNTING	FESTIVAL	LINCOLN	TRADITION
CELEBRATE	FLAG	MEMORIAL	VACATION
CHIEF	FLOATS	MONDAY	WASHINGTON
COMMEMORATION	FOUNDING	NATION	
COUNTRY	HISTORY	NOBLE	

Solution on page 299

Reference Works

```
E I D E T A R U C C A C G Q
S N I C G E B O L G A B U D
U S C R O D N H D T I O I E
R T T Y E M E I A B T B D S
U R I L C P P L L E W F E K
A U O A S L O I W N O B L R
S C N U O G O R L O O O E E
E T A T U G I P T A N O C F
H I R C R X T N E S T K T E
T V Y A C X O X E D N I R R
O E P F E T R A H C I Y O E
W H I T E P A P E R W A N N
Y A I S E C O N D A R Y I C
U C P A M S T N E T N O C E
```

ACCURATE	ELECTRONIC	ONLINE
BIBLIOGRAPHY	ENCYCLOPEDIA	QUOTE
BOOK	FACTUAL	REFERENCE
CATALOG	FOOTNOTES	REPORTS
CHART	GLOBE	SECONDARY
CITE	GUIDE	SOURCE
COMPILATION	INDEX	TEXT
CONTENTS	INSTRUCTIVE	THESAURUS
DESK	KNOWLEDGE	WHITE PAPER
DICTIONARY	MAP	

Solution on page 300

Attorneys

```
J U D G E O W I T N E S S T
C L I E N T R U O C Y R U J
D A M A G E S N E C I L O U
E R E C N E D I V E E D L S
F E D I S P U T E S K A I T
E D I V O R C E A N N N T I
N E A I R E B C O I O E I C
S F T L A W C W M I G O G E
E L I A B I L I T Y N P A C
S A O R D E R O T R I B N I
S I N E D C M R F C R U T F
I R N G B O O K S E A S Q F
O T E Y R E T A I N E R V O
N O T A R Y X O R P H S P Z
```

ACCIDENT	DISPUTE	LAW	PROXY
BAR	DIVORCE	LIABILITY	RETAINER
BOOKS	EVIDENCE	LICENSE	SESSION
CASE	FEDERAL	LITIGANT	SUBPOENA
CIVIL	FEES	MEDIATION	TRIAL
CLIENT	HEARING	MOTION	WITNESS
COURT	JUDGE	NOTARY	
CRIMINAL	JURY	OFFICE	
DAMAGES	JUSTICE	ORDER	
DEFENSE	KNOWLEDGE	PRACTICE	

Solution on page 300

Islands Everywhere

```
B O R N E O K I N A W A V V
R E T S A E T A S M A N I A
S T N I J I F N S L Y A C D
A S O G A P A L A G E N T A
R H A I T I L K D N N T O N
D I H F T O K E M O S U R E
I C U U T G L Y I K S C I R
N E E A O M A S R G O K A G
I L G R E E N L A N D E D H
A A U V F E D B L O A T U A
B N A D C W S A T H B A M W
U D M S I C I L Y A R V R A
R M A U R I T I U S A A E I
A B U C S A M A H A B J B I
```

ADMIRALTY	BORNEO	GUAM	NANTUCKET
ALEUTIAN	CAY	HAITI	OAHU
ARUBA	CUBA	HAWAII	OKINAWA
ASCENSION	EASTER	HONG KONG	SAMOA
ATOLLS	FALKLANDS	ICELAND	SARDINIA
BAHAMAS	FIJI	ISLET	SICILY
BALI	GALAPAGOS	JAVA	TASMANIA
BARBADOS	GREENLAND	KEYS	VICTORIA
BERMUDA	GRENADA	MAURITIUS	

Solution on page 300

Driving on the Freeway

```
E T S F D E D W O R C I L B
R C R S A C C E S S N A R S
T O I U A E E X I T N I N F
U N L C P L P E E D G A A R
R C E T O K R R S G I S V S
N R S D E P S E E S T R N P
P E R W I T L S D V W E O H
I T A E A C S S S N O D I A
K E C T I A C W P A U L T L
E U E H P R S A M C G U C T
N M E R G E R Y A I T O E O
D V E C I F F A R T A H R L
Q V M E D I A N B Y R S I L
O N E T U M M O C R O A D S
```

ACCESS	CONCRETE	MEDIAN	TAR
ACCIDENT	CROWDED	MERGE	TOLLS
ASPHALT	DIRECTION	OVERPASS	TRAFFIC
BARRIER	EXIT	POLICE	TRUCKS
BRIDGES	EXPRESSWAY	RAMPS	TURNPIKE
CARS	FAST	ROADS	UNDERPASS
CITY	GAS	ROUTE	VEHICLES
CLOVERLEAF	INTERSTATE	SHOULDERS	
COMMUTE	LANES	SIGNS	

Solution on page 300

See India

```
I Y R O T S I H D D U B J G
E P T H I N D U I S M S D A
R N O A D O O W Y L L O B D
U O U S H I M A L A Y A S Y
T I R I B T H S T R O S E R
N G I A S C E L E P H A N T
E I S L L A F R E T A W I S
V L T S A R N A I D N I R U
D E S E V T I S I V W T H D
A R C H I T E C T U R E S N
N A A C T A J M A H A L N I
C H V A S H O P P I N G P R
E I E E E P A C S D N A L A
J B S B F C O U N T R Y N S
```

ADVENTURE	DANCE	RELIGION
ARCHITECTURE	ELEPHANT	RESORTS
ASIA	FESTIVALS	SARI
ATTRACTIONS	HIMALAYAS	SEA
BEACHES	HINDUISM	SHOPPING
BIHAR	HISTORY	SHRINES
BOLLYWOOD	INDIAN	TAJ MAHAL
BUDDHIST	INDUSTRY	TOURISTS
CAVES	LANDSCAPE	VISIT
COUNTRY	NEW DELHI	WATERFALLS

Solution on page 301

Going Bananas

```
N N F R I E D P I L S N B U
I E B S E E D L E S S A X Y
K P E U I P O A M O N K E Y
S I G R N L O N G A O S K T
E R D D G C G T N D T P A H
D Y S O U T H A M E R I C A
I S W E E T P T T F E H S R
B N A T I U Q I H C S C O V
L A K P D W U O E T S A F E
E C U D O R P N A Z E N T S
E K I L F S E E R T D A G T
P N L T I L P S A N A N A B
G E L O D O O F R O V A L F
Y I L I S T E M A R E B I F
```

BANANA CHIPS	EDIBLE	MONKEY	SOFT
BANANA PUDDING	FIBER	PEEL	SOUTH AMERICA
BANANA SPLIT	FLAVOR	PIE	STEM
BUNCH	FOOD	PLANTATION	SWEET
CAKE	FRIED	PRODUCE	TREES
CHIQUITA	FRUIT	RIPEN	YELLOW
DESSERT	GOOD	SEEDLESS	
DOLE	GREEN	SKIN	
DRIED	HARVEST	SLIP	
EAT	LONG	SNACK	

Solution on page 301

Rhymes with Sue

```
V C N T Z L Z L T G C X D D
X B O F L E W B W V T R Y Q
N R H M O E B E O N A C F K
U U W B H T R A L D T B A C
F R E C Y D R I M B T Z F O
C I H S S Y S N H B O F O O
E W W T W V N T N O O H E G
W N E F E J O A E N S O S W
O W D K L V Q O D O C T P V
V E W G S I O U X I R W E D
W I Y R H H E M M E E E W L
F V O E A G U A W R W U W X
F L U W G U L H B E A L L E
J C Q J G H G S N A Q B A C
```

ADIEU	DEW	HUGH	STEW
BAMBOO	DREW	KAZOO	STREW
BLEW	EWE	NEW	TATTOO
BLUE	FEW	SCREW	THRU
BREW	FLEW	SHAMU	TWO
CANOE	FLU	SHOO	VIEW
CHEW	FONDUE	SIOUX	WAHOO
CLUE	GLUE	SKEW	WHEW
COO	GOO	SLEW	WHO
CUE	GREW	SPEW	YOU

Solution on page 301

Credit Cards

```
Y T F E H T Y F Y O T Y M W
I E T F R U L N R X G T Z N
K K N A B O A E K A B N A B
E C U O A P C W G C U M S U
C I O N M N X S C R E D I T
X Q C O A E B O W E A H V K
F O C L S R E B M U N H C Y
N L A R W U N G I S R N C M
G B U S A C I P N S P E N D
T P H O L E L I M I T R L B
R O X F L S N N T Y H O I C
P G T R E P O R T B G T A N
A O R A T E S W I P E S D D
E L B I L L L G H L H D O Y
```

ACCOUNT	CREDIT	NAME	SHOP
APR	DEBT	NUMBER	SIGN
BALANCE	FEE	ONLINE	SPEND
BANK	FRAUD	OWE	STORE
BILL	GOLD	PIN	SWIPE
BUY	ISSUER	PURSE	THEFT
CASH	LIMIT	RATES	THIN
CHARGE	LOAN	REPORT	TOTAL
CHECK	LOGO	SCORE	VISA
COMPANY	MONEY	SECURE	WALLET

Solution on page 301

Mining the Earth

```
C O A L G H S U R D L O G U
S L E N N U T V E I N S S R
D I G G I N G E P F N U H A
S E N O T S P X P F I O O N
M E I H S T E T O I A R V I
E C L T A E X R C C T E E U
T R L R L E C A R U N G L M
A U I A B L A C K L U N G Y
L O R E R O V T R T O A T T
A S D N O M A I D E M D L E
D E P O S I T O I L V F A F
T R U C K M I N E R A L S A
S A G E O L O G I C A L I S
A C C I D E N T S H A F T S
```

ACCIDENT	DIFFICULT	MINERALS	SILVER
BLACK LUNG	DIGGING	MOUNTAIN	STEEL
BLASTING	DRILLING	OIL	STONES
CART	EARTH	ORE	TRUCK
COAL	EXCAVATION	PIT	TUNNELS
COPPER	EXTRACTION	RESOURCE	URANIUM
DANGEROUS	GAS	SAFETY	VEIN
DEEP	GEOLOGICAL	SALT	
DEPOSIT	GOLD RUSH	SHAFTS	
DIAMONDS	METAL	SHOVEL	

Solution on page 302

Squash

```
H B R E B B U R F A S T J Y
I S C R O O D N I G N I W S
T V C T R U O C C I S N Y I
R P D O E N C O O S E R V E
O Y L H R C I P M Y L O Y M
P Q E A S E O L N R G D F A
S O G L Y I E M B E N O I G
G C P L L A L T P F I U L Q
N M L U G O G G L E S B F H
I A A U L V V X N R T L O B
R F E T O A T H L E T E N W
T E U Q C A R U L E S P Y
S J B N S H O E S P E E D R
L L A W C L U B A L L I K H
```

ATHLETE	GAME	OLYMPIC	SERVE
BALL	GOGGLES	PLAY	SHOES
BOUNCE	HIT	POINT	SINGLES
CLUB	INDOOR	POPULAR	SPEED
COMPETE	IOC	RACQUET	SPORT
COURT	KILL	RALLY	STRINGS
DOUBLES	LEAGUE	REFEREE	SWING
ENGLISH	LOB	RUBBER	TIN
FAST	MATCH	RULES	VOLLEY
FUN	NET	SCORE	WALL

Solution on page 302

Kelp Forest

```
G N I V I D E T C E T O R P
K T R O P I C A L J E L G A
L D V D H M O B E Y T I R C
A E I O A A S U V C A F O I
T N C O B C Y C I N R E W F
S S I F I R S S T A E A T I
A I T M T O T K C Y P H H C
O T A D A A E E U O M A C I
C Y U N T L M L D U E R R T
D D Q A P G S P O B T V A C
A L A S K A X B R K F E E R
L O B S T E R E P I T S S A
P C Q V H O L D F A S T E A
F R O N D S M S I N A G R O
```

ALASKA

ANIMALS

AQUATIC

ARCTIC

BUOYANCY

COASTAL

COLD

DENSITY

DIVING

ECOSYSTEM

FOOD

FRONDS

GIANT KELP

GROWTH

HABITAT

HARVEST

HOLDFAST

KELP BEDS

LIFE

LOBSTER

MACROALGAE

ORGANISMS

PACIFIC

PRODUCTIVE

PROTECTED

REEF

RESEARCH

SAND

SCUBA

STIPE

TEMPERATE

TROPICAL

Solution on page 302

Heavy Metal Music

```
S B D T A E B V I M A F M D
Q Q P M U A S O L H S J F P
O L O U S F C C S L E S D U
I W W S F O Z A B A V T I N
D V E I N L R L N M O A V K
A K R C M H Y S U A L G L C
R L E A T H E R K E U E Q O
L R B J T G D I I R M N Y R
T A U U N I D R O C E R V U
L J T U M R U P E S S E I O
O B R E G N A G C G G D D T
U G I W M R B A N D N N E X
D R A H T U O Y A E S I O N
Y C H Y S O U N D A R K S S
```

ALBUM	GUITAR	PARTY	STAGE
ANGER	HAIR	POWER	THRASH
BAND	HARD	PUNK	TOUR
BASS	JEANS	RADIO	VIDEOS
BEAT	KISS	RECORD	VOCALS
CONCERT	LEATHER	RIFFS	VOLUME
DANCE	LOUD	ROCK	YOUTH
DARK	LYRICS	SCREAM	
DRUM	METAL	SINGER	
GENRE	MUSIC	SONGS	
GRUNGE	NOISE	SOUND	

Solution on page 302

ANSWERS

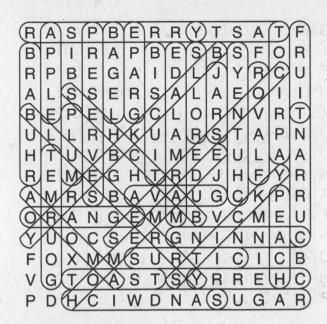

Jams and Jellies

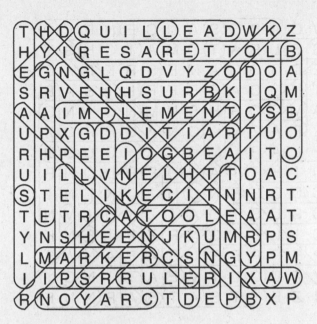

Writing Utensils

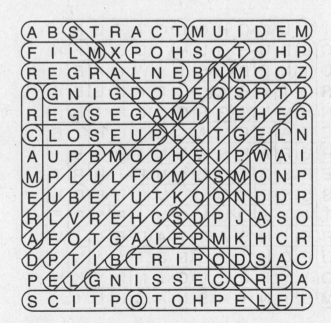

Photography Class

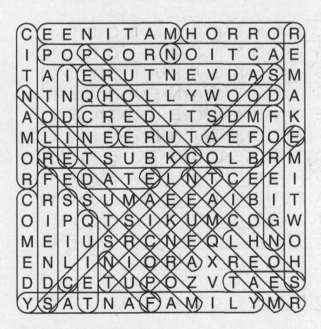

Going to the Movies

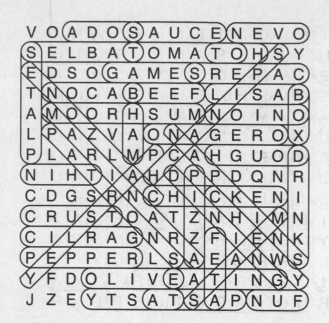

V O A D O S A U C E N E V O
S E L B A T O M A T O H S Y
E D S O G A M E S R E P A C
T N O C A B E E F L I S A B
A M O O R H S U M N O I N O
L P A Z V A O N A G E R O X
P L A R L M P C A H G U O D
N I H T I A H D P P D Q N R
C D G S R N C H I C K E N I
C R U S T O A T Z N H I M N
C I L R A G N R Z F I E N K
P E P P E R L S A E A N W S
Y F D O L I V E A T I N G Y
J Z E Y T S A T S A P N U F

Pizzeria

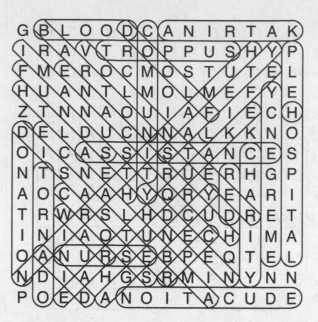

G B L O O D C A N I R T A K
I R A V T R O P P U S H Y P
F M E R O C M O S T U T E L
H U A N T L M O L M E F Y E
Z T N N A O U I A F I E C H
D E L D U C N N A L K K N O
O I C A S S I S T A N C E S
N T S N E T T R U E R H G P
A O C A A H Y O R Y E A R I
T R W R S L H D C U D R E T
I N I A O T U N E C H I M A
O A N U R S E B P E Q T E L
N D I A H G S R M I N Y N N
P O E D A N O I T A C U D E

Red Cross to the Rescue

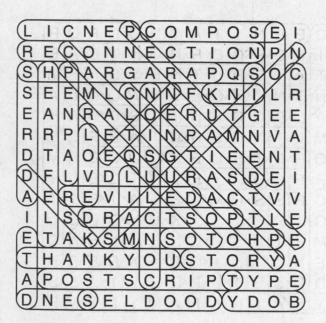

L I C N E P C O M P O S E I
R E C O N N E C T I O N P N
S H P A R G A R A P Q S O C
S E E M L C N N F K N I L R
E A N R A L O E R U T G E E
R R P L E T I N P A M N V A
D T A O E Q S G T I E E N T
D F L V D L U U R A S D E I
A E R E V I L E D A C T V V
I L S D R A C T S O P T L E
E T A K S M N S O T O H P E
T H A N K Y O U S T O R Y A
A P O S T S C R I P T Y P E
D N E S E L D O O D Y D O B

Write a Letter

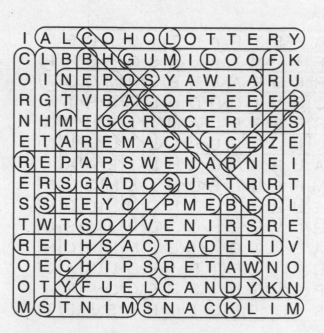

I A L C O H O L O T T E R Y
C L B B H G U M I D O O F K
O I N E P O S Y A W L A R U
R G T V B A C O F F E E E B
N H M E G G R O C E R I E S
E T A R E M A C L I C E Z E
R E P A P S W E N A R N E I
E R S G A D O S U F T R R T
S S E E Y O L P M E B E D L
T W T S O U V E N I R S R E
R E I H S A C T A D E L I V
O E C H I P S R E T A W N O
O T Y F U E L C A N D Y K N
M S T N I M S N A C K L I M

Convenience Store

246

Airport Runway

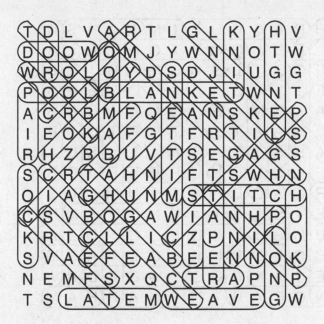

Knitting Needle

Educational

Words about Words

Eat a Sandwich

Around the Ocean

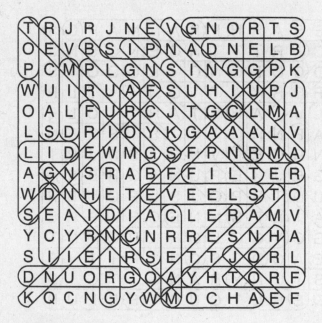

Cup of Coffee

Build a Rocket

248

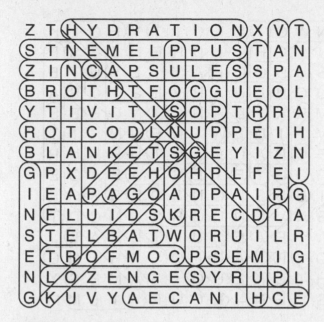

Cold Remedies

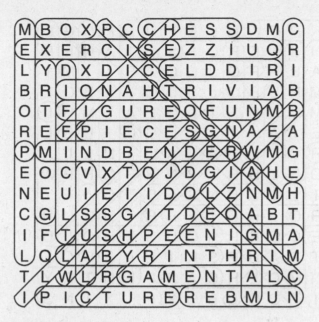

Puzzles

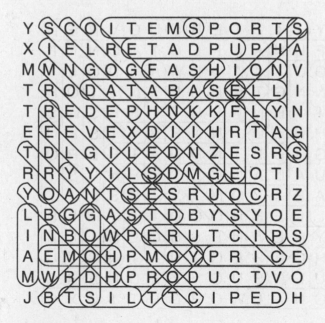

Catalogs

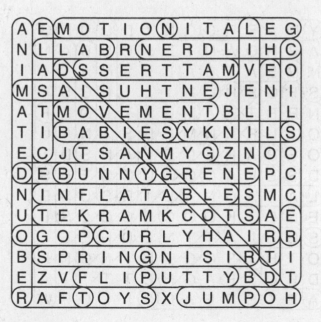

Bouncy

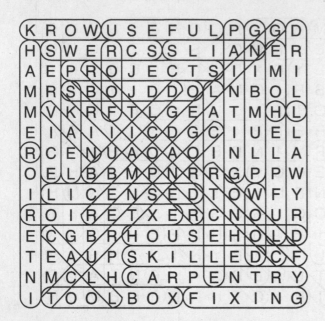

Hire Some Help

Festivals

Comfort Food

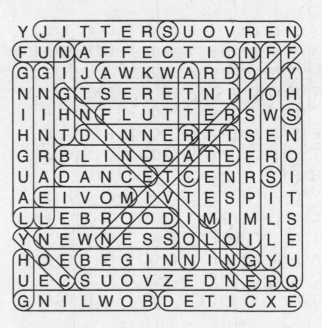

First Date

Fall

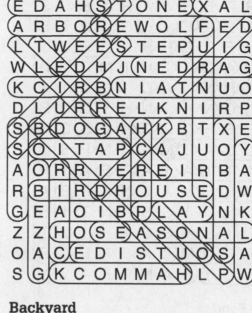

Backyard

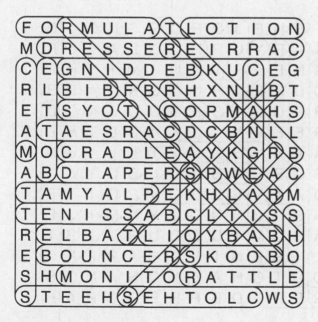

Baby Products

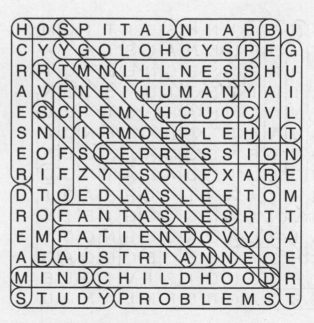

Psychiatric Therapy

Breakfast Food

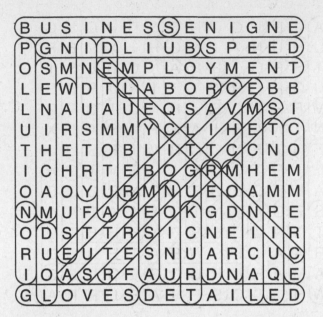

Industrial

Global Geography

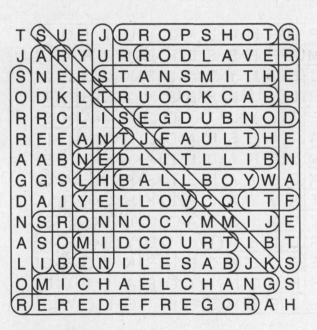

Tennis Player

252

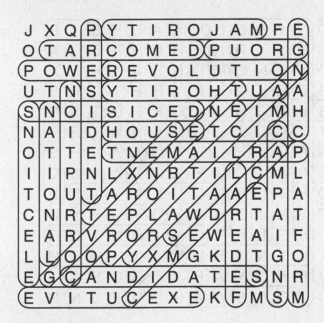

Political Life

Art History

On the Tube

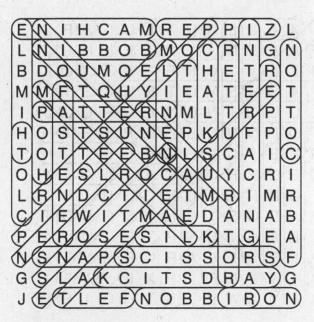

Sewing Supplies

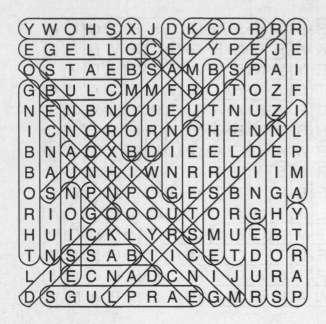

Loud Music

Casinos

Travel Abroad

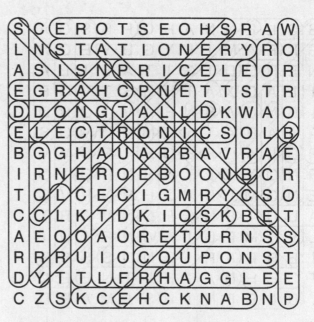

Going Shopping

Geological Study

Happy Anniversary

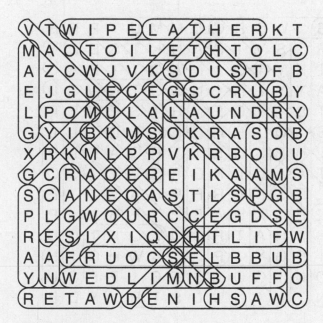

Housecleaning

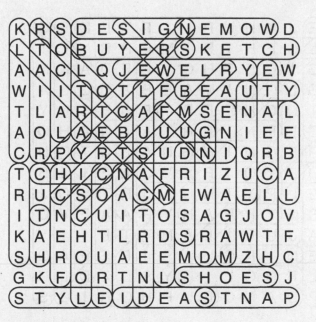

Fashion Design

Travel by Train

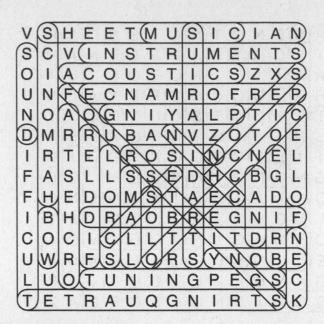

Play the Violin

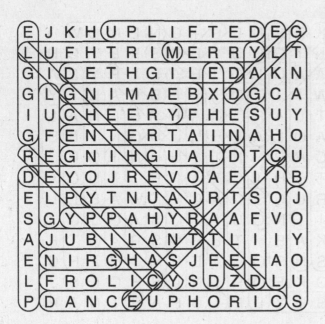

Gleeful

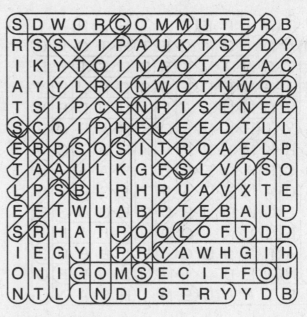

Urban Living

Museum Visit

Mountain Climbing

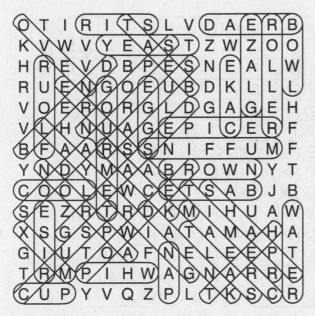

Baking

Managers at Work

Flower Shop

Autographs

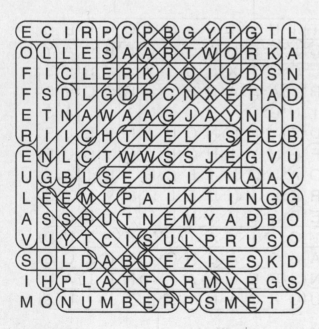

Auctions

At the Dentist

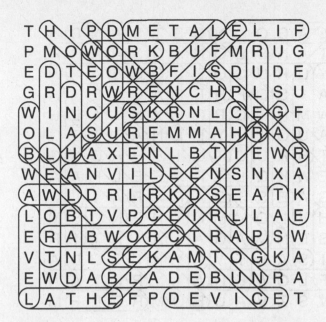

Tool

The International Space Station

Bar Scene

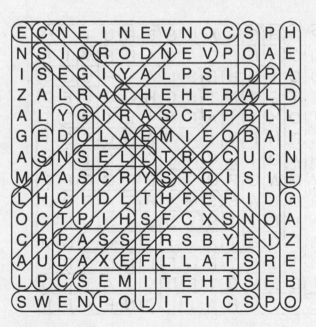

Newsstand

Listen to Jazz

Tropical

Scholars

Hands

Explore Outdoors

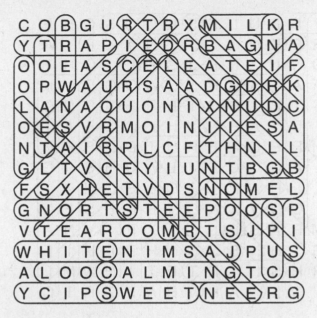

Cup of Tea

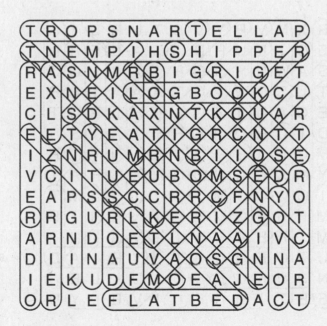

Trucker

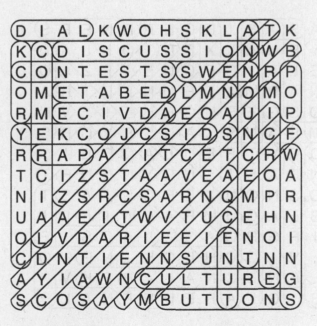

On the Radio

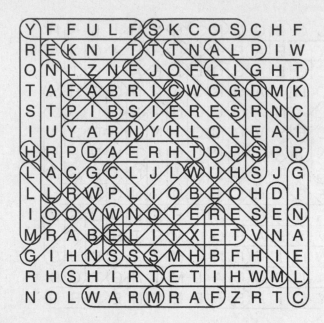

Made of Cotton

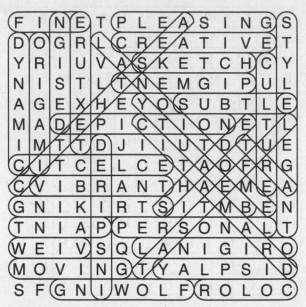

Artistic

Budgets

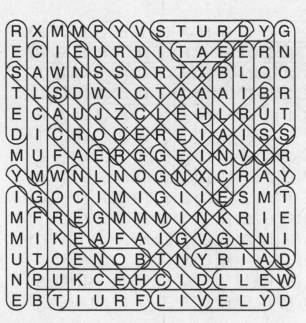

Healthy

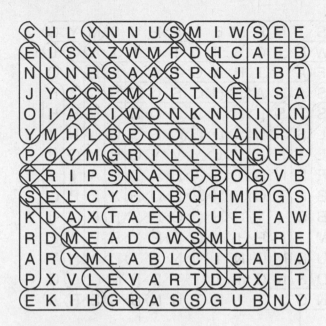

Summertime

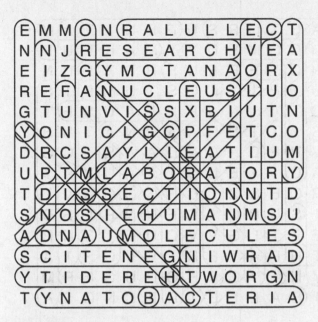

Basic Biology

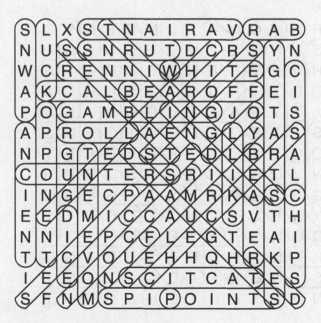

Playing Backgammon

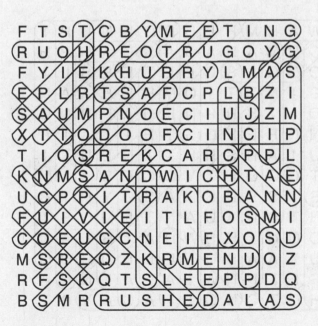

Lunchtime

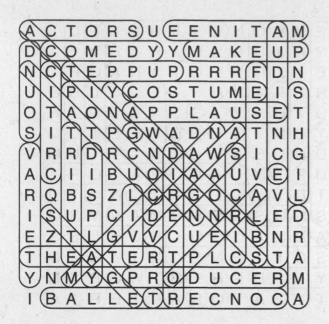

Shows

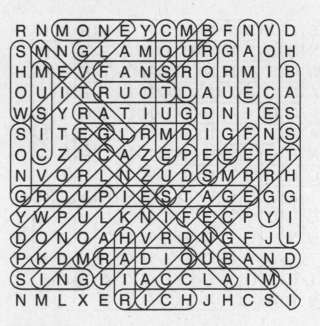

Bodybuilder

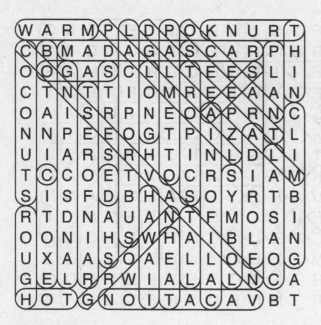

Palm Tree

Rock Star

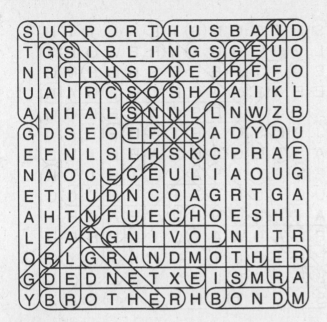

Family

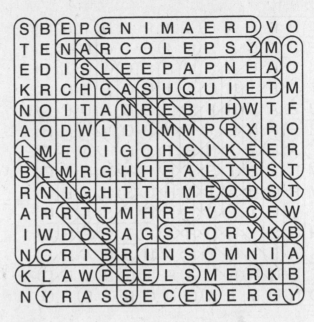

Sleep

Roller Skate

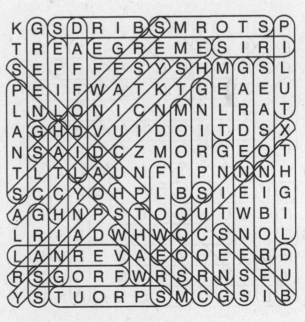

Spring Is in the Air

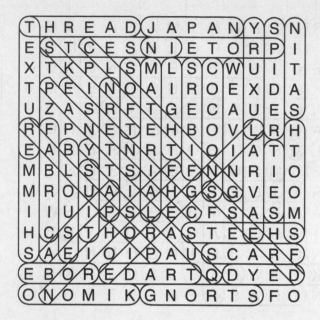

Made of Silk

Fast Cars

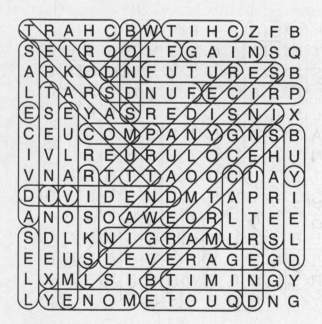

Stockbroker

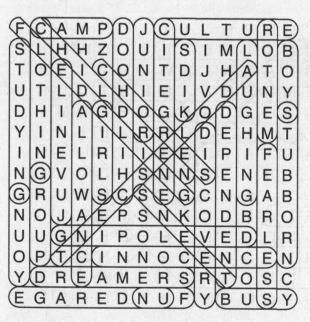

Youth

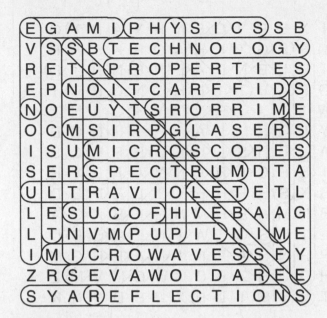

Optical

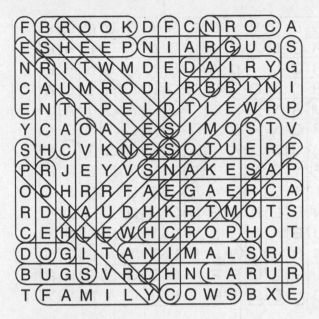

Country Life

Occupations

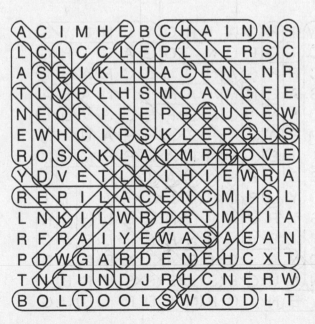

Hardware Store

Memorial Day

Waiter

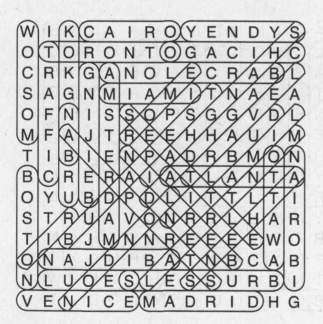

Cities Around the World

Ads Everywhere

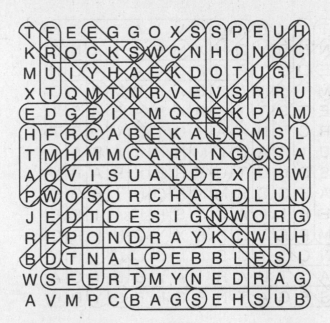

Landscaping

Buying a House

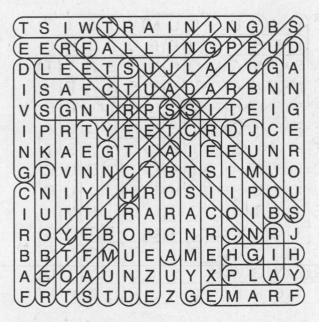

Jump on a Trampoline

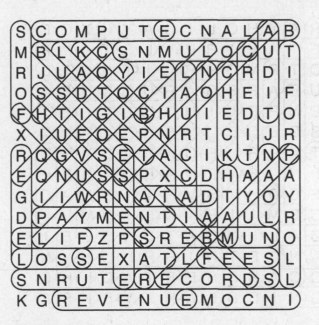

Accountant

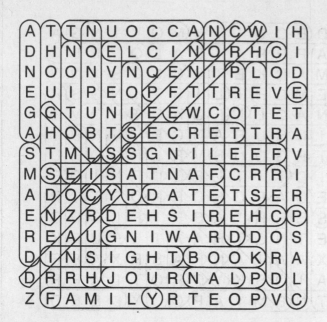

Dear Diary

Statistical Analysis

Invitation

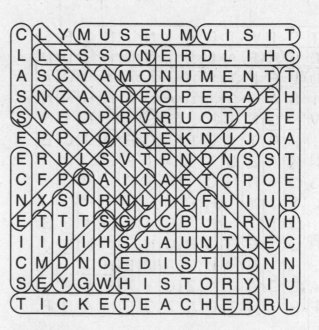

Field Trip

Corporate Culture

Weather Forecast

Gardener

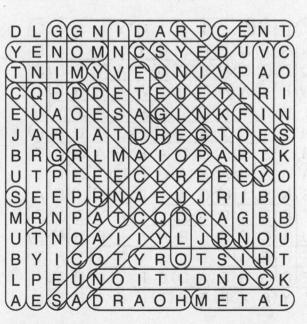

Collecting Coins

Kitchen Tools

Storage

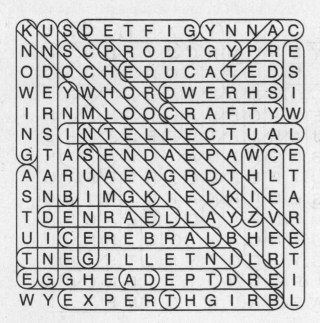

Smart Words

Mother's Day

Hooray for Hollywood

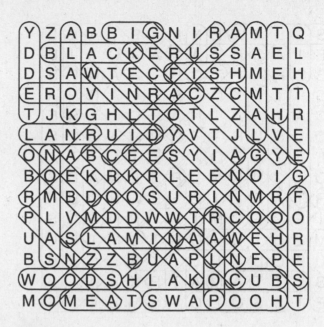

Bears

Paying the Bills

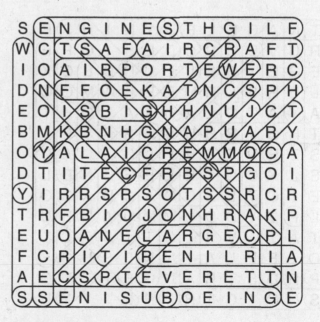

Boeing Jumbo Jet

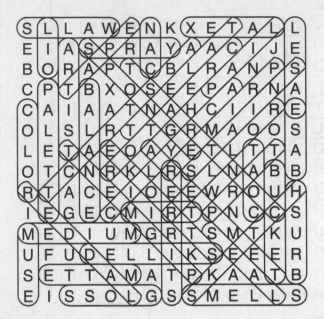

Painter

Public Transit

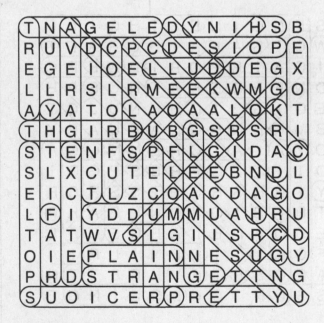

Appearances

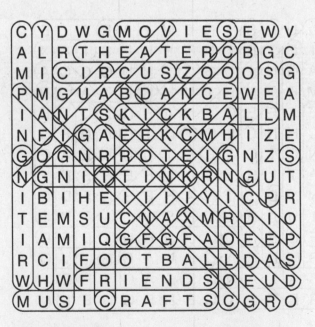

Fun Activities

274

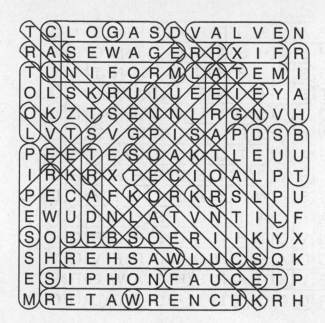

Plumber

Flea Market

Frightening

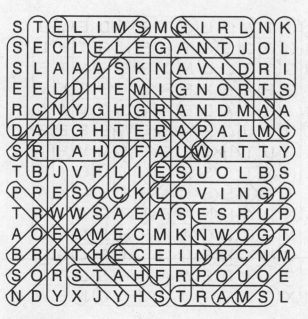

Women

Haircut

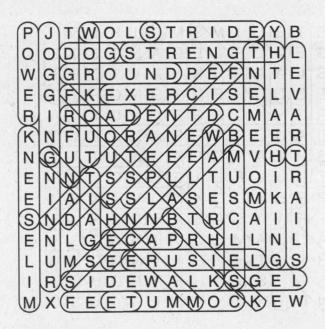

Walk Around

Dishwashing

Chewing Gum

Environment

Types of Music

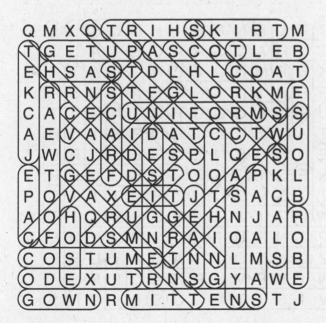

Apparel

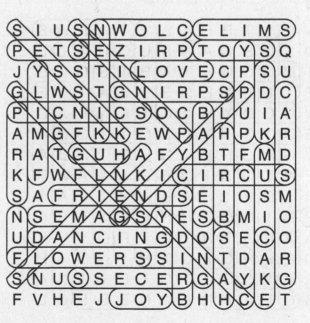

Happy Things

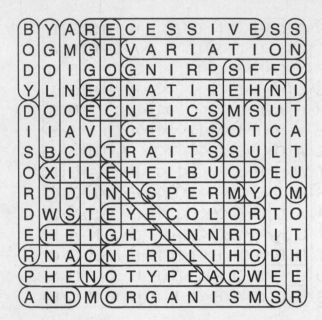

It's Genetic

Fish Tank

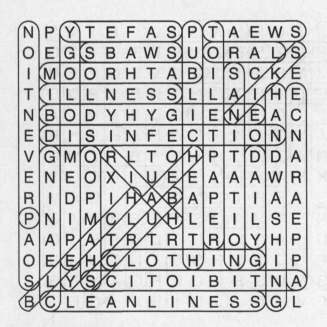

Keeping Clean

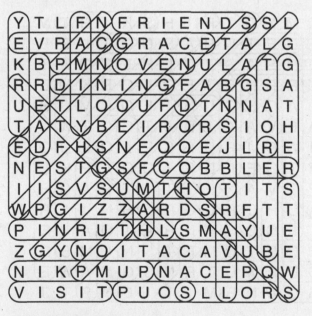

Thanksgiving Dinner

278

Computer Programs

Bank on It

Driving a Car

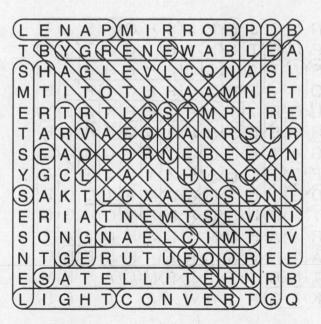

Solar Power

Collecting Things

Pests

Brewing Beer

Get Published

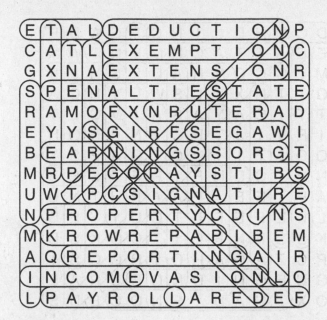

Tax Time

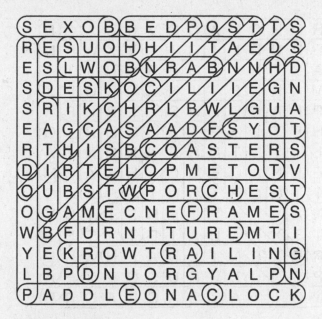

Made of Wood

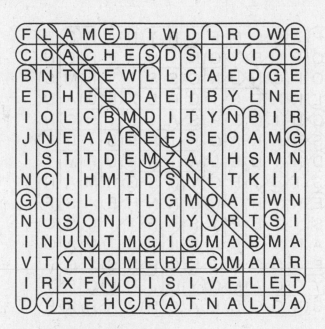

The Olympic Games

Symphony Orchestra

Media

True Friends

Take a Taxi

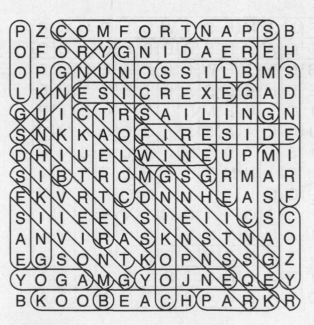

Relaxing

Father

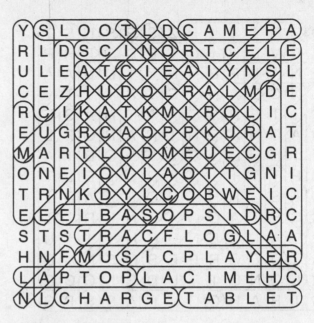

Battery-Powered

Aerospace

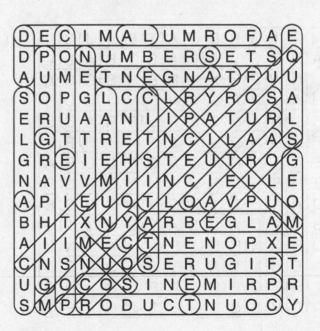

Math

Navigating

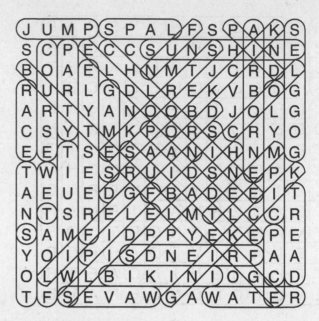

Jump in the Pool

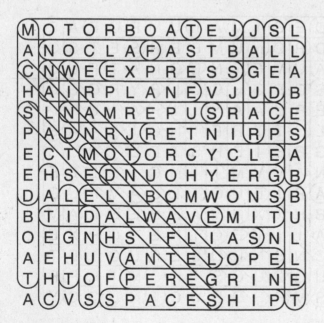

Fast Things

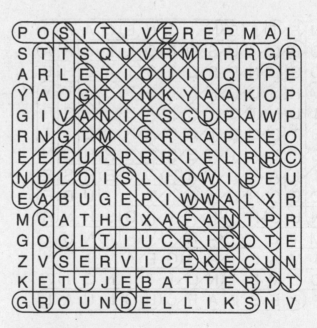

Electrician

284

Monosyllabic Words

Acting

Sites of the World

Laptop Computers

Halloween Party

Self-Help

Cool Things

Tent

In the Oven

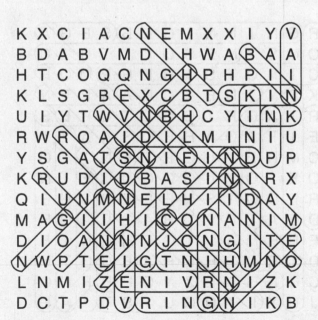

IN Words

Salty

Neighbors

Farmers

```
R Y R T L U O P M C K X B Q
F W E M E R U T S A P X N X
H R R F G M U D L E I F L E
L A U A N I M A L S G J L S
F E N I V O B T R O U G H R
N I A M T K T H R E S H J U
C R M S F A L L O W T E S R
O K A G C E R I S W A L A A
W X R B M B N P M N O N O L
O H K O Z I O C S P G L H B
O A E U W R N O E E I O P I
L Y T A C B E E T S R T U B
E S K E T F H N D S D E E S
M D Q F L S Y I E L D R I Z
```

Romance

```
S E L I M S T R A E H U G T
E L E V A R T R U O C S U G
V F R O S E S C I S U M N I
O E G O O W H H P D D E I F
D E N A M O R E D N E O T T
A L I E R L S R E O V P E S
T I N M A F E I U M O A D R
E N R O H W R G A T I S O A
T G A T C F E H I I I S T T
A S E I Y L N E R D O I S I
D S Y O D I A D T F N O N L
O I B N N R D A N C I N G O
R K A S O T E D I N I N G V
E C A R B M E S O P O R P E
```

Fried Food

```
D D E L I C I O U S C Y W E
A S E I R O L A C O I U O L
E E S E I R F Y R L R M N Z
R O A M P I D N L T A M T Z
B T U G O F D O C A M Y O I
U A S N W O R B H S A H N S
R T A I G G R Y E T L T S K
G O G N G T O H E Y A L H E
E P E E C I R R S R C A R W
R B A T T E R K E U Q E I E
S E O T A M O T R T M H M R
D J S A L L I T R O T N P N
H S I F S A L T E M P U R A
H E S A E R G J N O C A B P
```

Ancient History

```
R G N I N N I G E B S E G A
O M S Y M E S O L I T H I C
C I R O T S I H E R P M O H
K P Y T N E I C N A A P T N
R T A G R I C U L T U R E S
E I F S O A H E O S A A Y T
C M R L T L O P T E N I T O
O E I O Y L O O G D C E I N
R P C O I S N E E P G U E H
D E A T E E O R A O D A Q H
E R H M A L T G C H R N I E
D I R G O H E H A E C O T N
C O E G A E Z N O R B R N G
J D Y L I N G U I S T I A E
```

Surfing the Internet

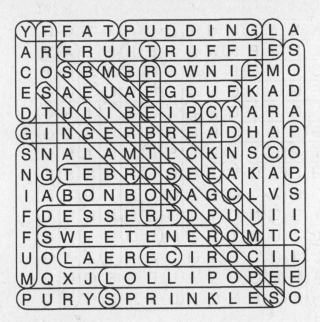

Sweet Tooth

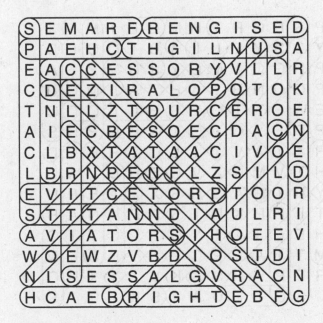

Wear Sunglasses

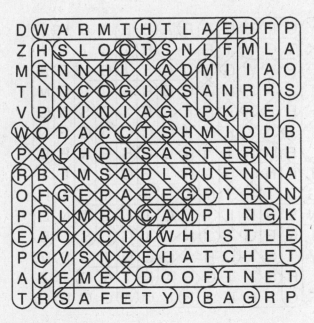

Survival Kit

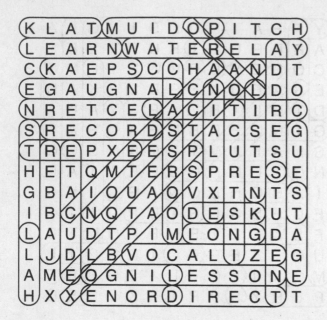

Lecture

Lighting Up the House

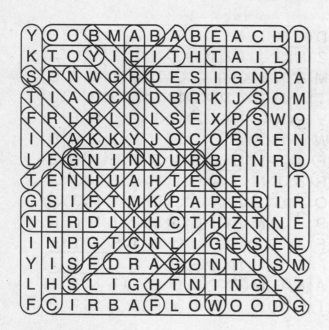

Kites in the Sky

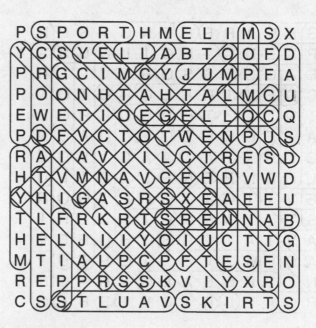

Cheerleaders

Riding the Subway

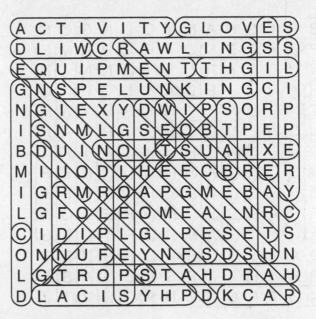

Cave Adventure

Dining Room

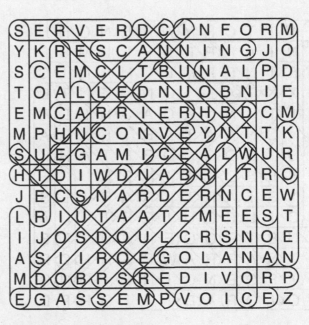

Telecommunications

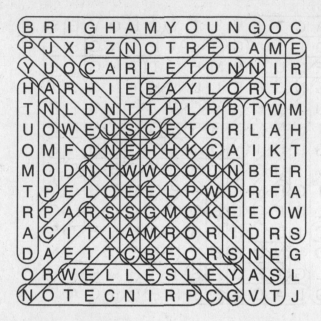

College Choices

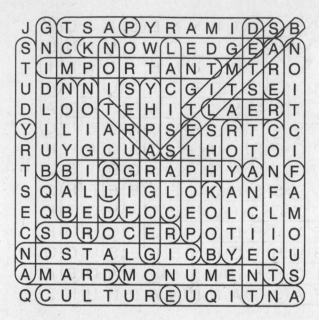

Historical

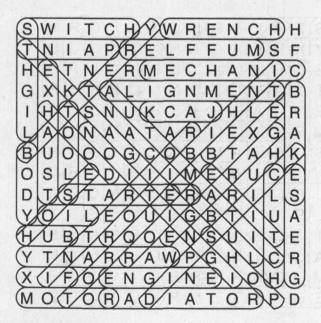

Auto Repair

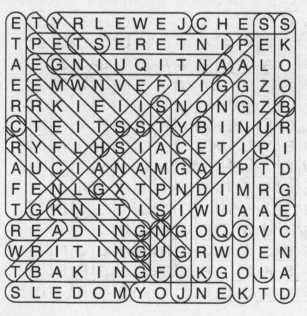

Hobby

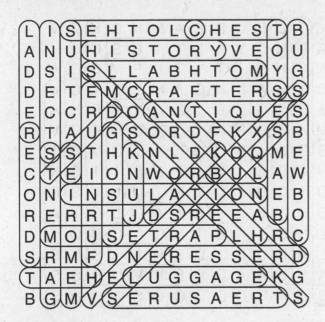

In the Attic

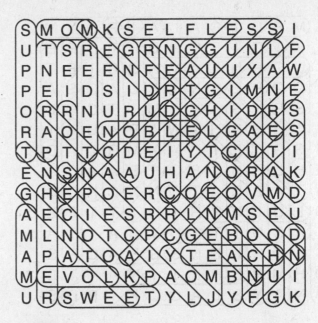

Mother

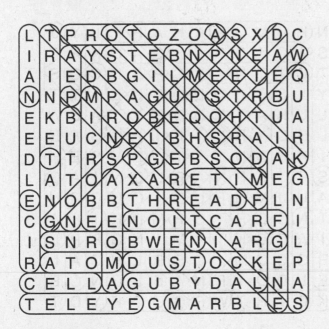

Tiny Things

Front Porch

Optometrist

Fun at the Fair

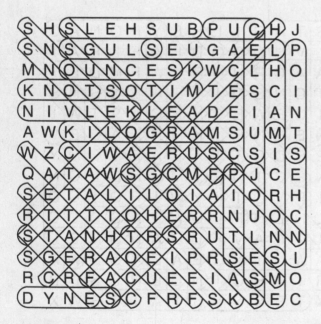

Measuring

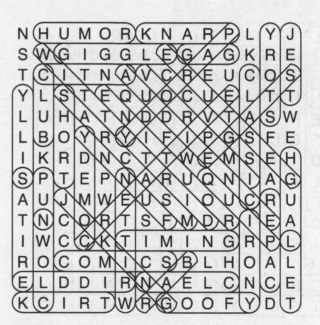

Jokes

Creative Writing

Slow Things

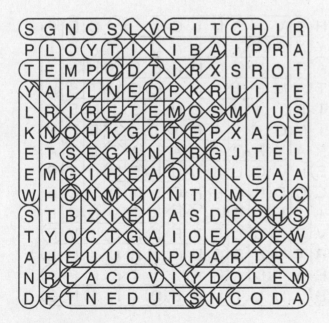

Music Lessons

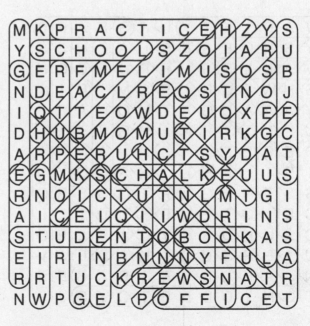

Teaching

All Kinds of Floors

Fancy Handwriting

Department Stores

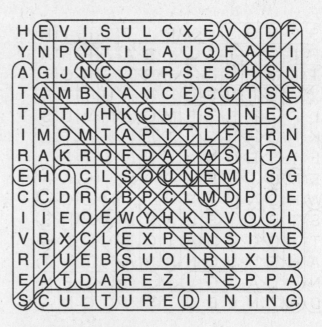

Fancy Restaurant

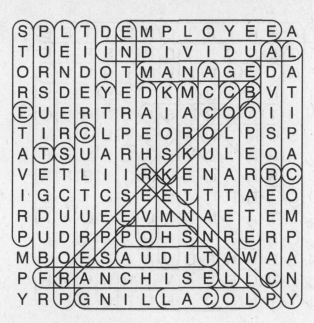

Bedroom

Small Business

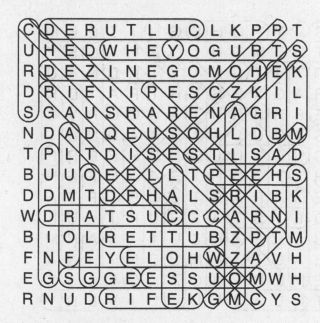

Dairy Products

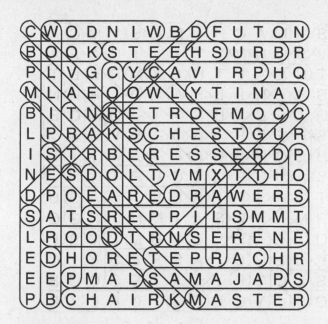

Researching

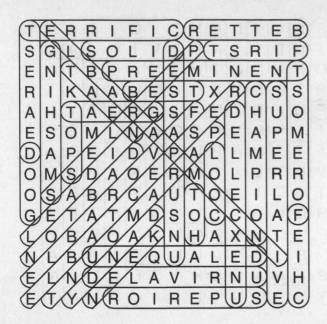

Great Words

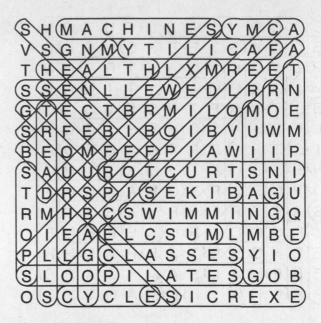

Fitness Club

Faces

Running Errands

Wealthy

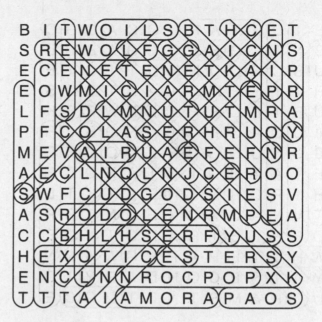

Fragrance

Recycle Things

Presidents' Day

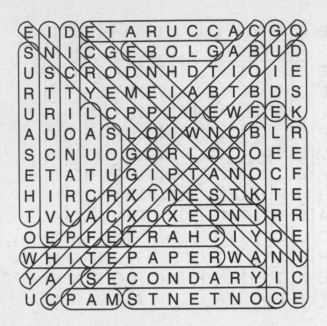

Reference Works

Attorneys

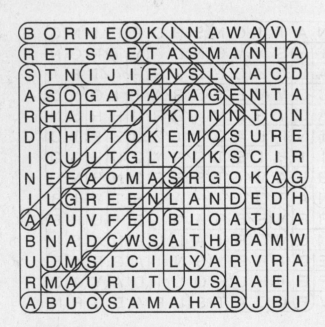

Islands Everywhere

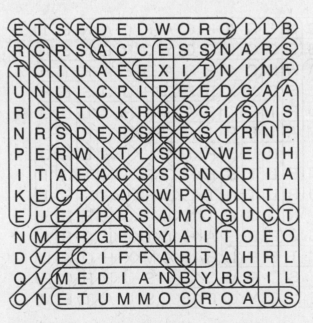

Driving on the Freeway

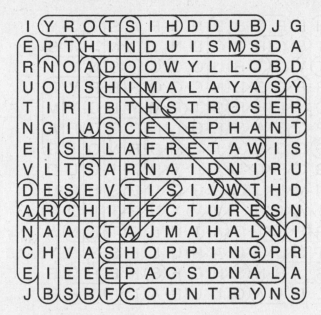

See India

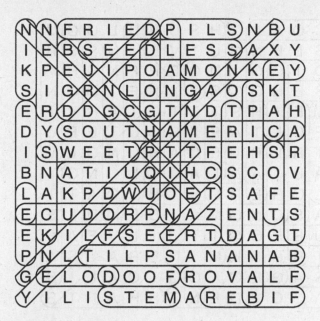

Going Bananas

Rhymes with Sue

Credit Cards

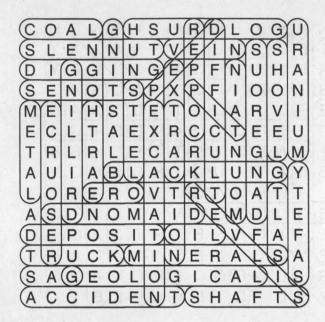

Mining the Earth

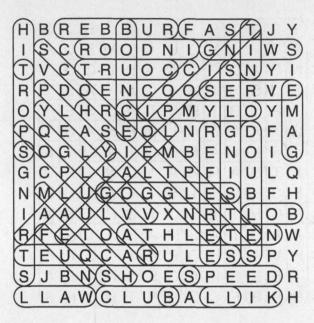

Squash

Kelp Forest

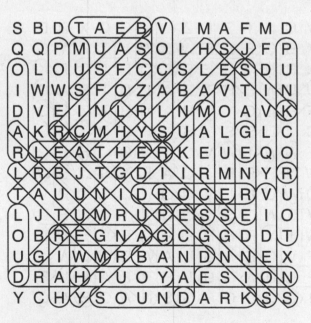

Heavy Metal Music

We Have EVERYTHING® on Anything!

With more than 19 million copies sold, the Everything® series has become one of America's favorite resources for solving problems, learning new skills, and organizing lives. Our brand is not only recognizable—it's also welcomed.

The series is a hand-in-hand partner for people who are ready to tackle new subjects—like you!

For more information on the Everything® series, please visit *www.adamsmedia.com*

The Everything® list spans a wide range of subjects, with more than 500 titles covering 25 different categories:

Business	History	Reference
Careers	Home Improvement	Religion
Children's Storybooks	Everything Kids	Self-Help
Computers	Languages	Sports & Fitness
Cooking	Music	Travel
Crafts and Hobbies	New Age	Wedding
Education/Schools	Parenting	Writing
Games and Puzzles	Personal Finance	
Health	Pets	